"Dr. Edward Dalcour's book, An Introduction to Christian Apologetics: Necessity and Purpose, is precisely what the title indicates: a sound and Scriptural defense of the Christian faith, showing both in its necessity and purpose. Having engaged Dr. Dalcour in private conversation about these and other biblical matters, I'm grateful that he has put into print these basic principles of apologetics, especially for the benefit of those beginners who desire some sure-footing on how to both think about—and to defend—the Christian faith. Having for many years engaged in speaking and writing regarding the defense of Christianity, both Dr. Dalcour and I believe that Scripture is always our best and most powerful tool of defense, since God Himself—through His inerrant Word—proclaims the truth of Himself as no other can or does. May this introductory guide help you therefore take God's Word to heart, believing that it is the very power of God unto salvation in Jesus Christ!"

~ **Lance Quinn**, Ph.D., Evangelical Theological Faculty, Leuven, Belgium; contributing author of The Five Points of Calvinism: Defined, Defended and Documented.

"Apologetics has remained the missing link in Christian evangelism for far too long. Not knowing why we believe what we believe has had disastrous consequences in the church not only in the past but more so in the present. In this very helpful book Dr. Dalcour presents the reader with an accessible approach to apologetics and why it is vitally important not only in the defense of the gospel but its proclamation. Various topics related to the field of apologetics are addressed in this book that every Christian would benefit in learning to apply in their witness. I highly recommend this book as a helpful introduction to apologetics."

~ **Tony Costa**, Ph.D., Toronto Baptist Seminary

"While every Christian is commanded in the Bible to evangelize, and defend the faith they embrace, not every believer understands what that commandment means, or how to honor the will of the Lord in this area. Dr. Edward Dalcour has written a practical book that exhorts the believer to boldly be a Christian apologist, while providing basic material which is needed to be an effective communicator of the gospel. In an ever-increasing hostile world towards Christians, An Introduction to Christian Apologetics: Necessity and Purpose is a useful book to study carefully, and often. The wealth of condensed Biblical truths contained in each chapter can be appropriately used when discussing Apologetics, the Trinity, Jesus as the Son of God, the Reliability of the New Testament, or the danger of believing in Another Jesus. In every cult and false religion, Jesus is consistently and inadequately presented. Dr. Dalcour's grasp of the Greek language is impressive, scholarly, and faithful to the Scriptures. I highly recommend this book be read by every Christian in order to be ready and willing to contend earnestly for the faith which was once for all handed down to the saints."

~ **Stanford E. Murrell,** Th.D., Founder
of Redeeming Grace Ministries

"I highly recommend this introductory book by Dr. Dalcour to all who want to be informed and equipped to proclaim and defend the faith once for all entrusted unto the saints."

~ **Rev. Anthony Rogers,** PCA, Regional
Director SC, Metanoia Prison Ministry

"In his An Introduction to Christian Apologetics, Dr. Edward Dalcour has produced an outstanding primer on apologetics. This volume is both accessible and helpful; affording its readers exegetical depth and sound method. Highly recommended."

~ **Rev. Michael R. Burgos,** Ph.D., President,
Forge Theological Seminary

AN INTRODUCTION TO

CHRISTIAN APOLOGETICS

Necessity and Purpose

EDWARD L. DALCOUR
M.Apol., Ph.D.

FirstLove Publications
P.O. Box 588
Baghdad, FL 32530

www.firstloveministries.org

Published in the United States by FirstLove Publications

ISBN: 978-1-953151-35-3

For copies of this book or a catalog write to:

FirstLove Publications
P.O. Box 588
Baghdad, FL 32530

Visit our website to download this publication free of
charge, and to order Christian literature on various topics:
www.firstlovepublications.org

Comments are welcome by writing to the above address.

Contents

ONE

Apologetics Necessity & Purpose

"I know your deeds and your labor and perseverance, and that you cannot tolerate evil people, and you have put those who call themselves apostles to the test, and they are not, and you found them to be **false**; [3] and you have perseverance and have endured on account of My name, and have not become weary" (Rev. 2:2-3).

The biblical mandate of every believer (esp. to those in Christian ministry positions, viz. pastors, teachers, evangelists) is to grow theologically (2 Pet. 3:18), contend for and defend the faith (1 Pet. 3:15; Jude 1:3), and to evangelize (Rom. 1:16; 10:15, 17)—in obedience to the Lord.

APOLOGETICS DEFINITION

The term "apologetics" comes from the Greek noun *apologia* (in all case

1

forms), which appears eight times in the Greek NT. The term *apologia* is a compound word from *apo* ("from") and *logos* (logic/intelligent reasoning"), thus, to provide an answer or logical and coherent response to an objection raised. It is an intelligent verbal defense, or speech. The term was used in an ancient court for making a legal defense.

BIBLICAL APPLICATION

1 Peter 3:15: "But sanctify Christ as Lord in your hearts, always being ready to make a defense [*apologian*] to everyone who asks you to give an account for the hope that is in you, yet with gentleness and reverence." As with the book of James, 1-3 John, Jude, and Peter's Epistles are "catholic" Epistles, meaning general or universal letters. Unlike the narrative books (Gospels, Acts), the NT general Epistles were not written to particular churches or persons; rather, they were to the general population of Christians. In this passage, the commandment, to all Christians, starts with sanctifying Jesus Christ as Lord in one's heart.[1] The verb *hagiasate* ("sanctify") is in the aorist imperative, indicating an urgent command.[2] This is the only commandment in the passage. In verses 14 and the first part of 15, Peter draws from the LXX (Septuagint[3]) of Isaiah 8:12-13 in which the first part of verse 13 reads: *Kurion auton hagiasate* ("[the] Lord Himself sanctify"), translated from the Hebrew phrase: "The LORD [YHWH] of Host, He you must sanctify." So, in 1 Peter 3:15, Peter sees Christ as the *Kurion* ("Lord"), that is, the YHWH of Isaiah 8:13 that must be sanctified/set apart. Peter even uses the same aorist imperative verb *hagiasate* as in the LXX of Isaiah 8:13.

According to Peter, apologetics starts with the commandment (the only commandment in the passage) to sanctify the Lord Jesus in one's heart.

---

1   Based in the Critical Text (CT, or Eclectic Text, the Nestle-Aland 28th ed., and UBS 5th ed.). The CT however, is the current Greek NT edition from which most modern translations are based. Even between the Majority Text and CT, there exists only about 6,600 differences (Wallace). Both editions are in 95% agreement, which is about 4.7% variation between these editions (Ibid). None of the variants in the Greek NT editions affect any major Christian doctrine.

2   The imperative mood signifies a commandment. However, when the imperative is in the aorist tense, it denotes the strongest way in Greek to issue a command.

3   The LXX is the abbreviation for the Septuagint (from the Latin, *septuaginta* meaning "seventy"). Seventy was the traditional number of scholars that translated the OT Hebrew into Greek. The LXX originated in Alexandria, Egypt and was translated between 300-200 B.C. The NT authors greatly utilized the LXX. In fact, virtually all of the OT citations contained in the book of Hebrews were taken from the LXX.

Consider the following points:

1. **"Always being ready to make a *defense*" (*apologia*).** The term translated "defense" is *apologia,* which is a verbal intelligent defense, or speech. In the Classical period it was used as a legal term. All Christians are called to defend the faith, not by philosophy, but rather by Scripture.

2. **"Give a *reason*" (*logos*)** for that defense, with gentleness and respect. Apologetics then is a "reasonable defense" of essential biblical theology in which the entire Christian faith rests. In an age where apologetics and essential doctrine become a mere sidebar in the Christian church, it was a primary theme in the Scriptures. The Apostle Paul, for example, devotes enormous space in his letters to the defense and proclamation of the gospel. In fact, virtually all of the NT Epistles were written to combat deception, allowing the church to refute (defend against) false doctrines.4 And affirming essential truths of the gospel such as the hypostatic union of Christ (as God-man), the triune concept of God, the physical resurrection of Christ, and justification through faith alone apart from works, the effects of original sin, etc.

Acts 17:16-17—Paul in Athens: **16 "Now while Paul was waiting for them at Athens, his spirit was being provoked within him as he was observing the city full of idols."** The term "provoked" (*paroxunō*) carries the meaning to incite or jab someone or something. Thayer defines the meaning as "to irritate, provoke, rouse to anger; to stimulate their emotions."5 The verb here is an imperfect indicative denoting a repeated action. Paul's provocation against the idolatry he saw was persistent and ongoing.

17 "So [as a result] he reasoned in the synagogue with the Jews and the devout persons, and in the marketplace every day with those who happened to be there." The term "reasoned" is from the Greek

---

4 Also, Paul presented polemics, that is, he "yanked down" (2 Cor. 10:5) and destroyed arguments against the faith. Apologetics defends biblical truth and speaks of the truthfulness of the Christian faith. Whereas polemics argues against a non-Christian world view, which opposes the Christian faith. Broadly speaking, both apologetics and polemics are **essentially** an analysis and critique of any opposing position to Christian doctrine.

5 Joseph H. Thayer, *Thayer's Greek-English Lexicon of the New Testament* (1896; reprint, with Strong's numbering added by Hendrickson Publishers, Peabody, MA, 1996).

word *dialegomai*. This term is a compound word from *dia* ("through") and *legō* ("to reason, speak"). Also, the verb is in the imperfect tense6 indicating that the action of "reasoning" was an ongoing past repeated action, not a mere one-time occurrence with Paul. So, what was Paul arguing? Note Acts 17:2-3:

> [2] And according to Paul's custom, he went to them, and for three Sabbaths reasoned with them from the Scriptures, [3] explaining and giving evidence that the Christ had to suffer and rise again from the dead, and saying, "This Jesus whom I am proclaiming to you is the Christ.

Acts 18:28: "For he [Apollos] powerfully refuted the Jews in public, demonstrating by the Scriptures that Jesus was the Christ" (cf. vv. 24-27).

Philippians 1:7, 16. Writing from prison (house arrest), Paul explained to the church of Philippi that "it was because of "apologetics" that he was in chains: [7] "Since both in my imprisonment and in the defense [*apologia*] and confirmation of the gospel, you all are partakers of grace with me.... [16] I am appointed for the defense [*apologian*] of the gospel."

Jude 1:3: "Beloved, while I was making every effort to write you about our common salvation, I felt the necessity to write to you appealing that you contend earnestly for the faith which was once for all handed down to the saints."

As with 1 Peter 3:15, Jude, through the Holy Spirit, instructs all Christians to "contend earnestly for the faith which was **once for all** [*hapax*] handed down [delivered] to the saints" (Matt. 7:15, 21-27; 2 Cor. 10:3-5; Titus 1:9, 13).

THE GLORY OF GOD IN APOLOGETICS: THE CHURCH OF EPHESUS

While Paul was meeting with the Ephesian pastors (elders), he gave

---

6 *Dielegeto* from the base verb, *dialegomai*. Thus, Paul kept reasoning.

them pointed instructions of their divine calling as pastors of the church (Acts 20:17:31). In verses 26-31 we read:

> [26] Therefore, I testify to you this day that I am innocent of the blood of all men. [27] For I did not shrink from declaring to you the whole purpose of God. [28] Be on guard for yourselves and for all the flock, among which the Holy Spirit has made you overseers, to shepherd the church of God, which He purchased with His own blood. [29] I know that after my departure savage wolves will come in among you, not sparing the flock; [30] and from among your ownselves men will arise, speaking perverse things, to draw away the disciples after them. [31] Therefore be on the alert, remembering that night and day for a period of three years I did not cease to admonish each one with tears.

Paul's central admonishment to the overseers (semantically synonymous with *elders, pastors*) of the church was to "Be on guard for yourselves and for all the flock" (v. 28); against the "false teachers" (savage wolves) within the church (vv. 29-30); "Therefore be on the alert" (v. 31). Question: Did the Ephesian overseers (pastors) listen? Yes they did! Look at Jesus' message to them in Revelation 2:2-3:

> [2] "I know your deeds and your **toil** [*kopon*] and perseverance, and that you cannot tolerate evil men, and you put to the test those who call themselves apostles, and they are not, and you found them to be false; [3] and you have perseverance and have endured for My name's sake, and have not grown weary."

Jesus says He knows (*oida*) their deeds/works. Jesus sees all in the church and each member, in and out. The term "toil" is from the Greek noun *kopos* meaning, "toil of labor," intense laborious work, involving fatigue – from the verb *koptō*, to hit, denoting deep fatigue; "to cut, by means of a sharp-edged instrument (BDAG7). Thayer indicates that the *kopos* is equivalent to *koptein* in Jeremiah 51:33 (LXX): A beating of the breast in grief or sorrow; intense labor. In the NT, *kopos* is synonymous with *ponos*, which carries the meaning of "pain" as in Revelation 21:4. Jesus commended the church of Ephesus for their intense painful labor and perseverance in 1) not tolerating evil men (false teachers), 2) testing those who call themselves apostles, who were not, 3) finding them false, and 4) enduring for Jesus' name sake and not growing weary. They glorified God in their deeds of continuous and laborious apologetics adhering to Paul's warning of the wolves "from among your own selves" (i.e., in the church). The Apostle Paul's entire Christian life was defending and affirming the essential doctrines of the Christian faith (the gospel).

APOLOGETIC DUTY FOR CHRISTIANS

What is our biblical obligation when we encounter false teachings or teachers? Jesus commanded in Matthew 7:15: "Beware8 of the false prophets, who come to you in sheep's clothing, but inwardly are ravenous wolves" (cf. 7:21-27).

HAVING A SET-FOUNDATION

Accurately defending and affirming the truth requires that one is familiar with the truth. If one is not familiar with the basic truth of the gospel, how is he or she going to be familiar with teachings that oppose biblical truth? In 2 Timothy 2:15, Paul stresses directly to the pastors: **"Be diligent to present yourself approved to God as a workman who does not need to be ashamed, accurately handling the word of truth."** Although written directly to pastors, all Christians should make every effort to handle God's Word accurately and precisely ensuring with great diligence that their interpretation is correct before they apply it to themselves and others. The first phrase, "Be diligent" is from the verb, *spoudason*, which is in the aorist imperative (from

---

7   Walter Bauer's, *A Greek English Lexicon of the New Testament and Other Early Christian Literature*, 3rd ed., ed. and rev. by Frederick W. Danker [hereafter BDAG] (Chicago, IL: University of Chicago, 2000).

8   The term "beware" (*prosechete*) is a present imperative, thus, a commandment, not a suggestion.

spoudazō)—namely, as seen above, stressing urgency. The verb carries the meaning of being swift or fast, "to exert oneself" (Thayer). It stresses especially to pastors to "be zealous/eager, take pains, make every effort" (BDAG). Pastors and church leaders have a higher responsibility to defend and refute false teachers and doctrines (Titus 1:9, 13). The phrase, "accurately handling" is from the verb *orthotomounta*, which is a present active participle (of *orthotomeō*, lit., "to cut straight"!). The present participle indicates the *continuous action* of accurately handling the Scripture. After Paul affirms the sufficiency of *Scripture alone* for the task of teaching, rebuking, correcting, "training in righteousness" and equipping the man of God for *pan ergon agathon* ("every good work," 2 Tim. 3:16-17), he furthers instructs pastors to: "Preach the word; be ready in season and out of season; correct, rebuke, and exhort, with great patience and instruction" (2 Tim. 4:2). Note the five aorist imperatives (stressing urgency): *Preach, be ready, reprove/refute, rebuke,* and *exhort/encourage.* Why is Paul stressing such urgency of these commandments? Paul states the reasons in the next verses, 3-4:

> [3] For the time will come when they will not endure sound doctrine; but wanting to have their ears tickled, they will accumulate for themselves teachers in accordance to their own desires, [4] and will turn away their ears from the truth and will turn aside to myths.

Affirming and defending the faith was commanded and/or practiced by **Jesus** (Matt. 7:15); **Paul** (Acts 20:17-31; Gal. 1:6, 8; Col. 2:3-4, 8-9; Titus 2:13); **Peter** (1 Pet. 3:15; 2 Pet. 2:1ff.); **Jude** (Jude 1:3); and **John** (1ˢᵗ and 2ⁿᵈ John). As said, virtually every NT Epistle was written for the express purpose of refuting false doctrines and providing a positive affirmation of essential truth. In John 20:31, the Apostle John provides a two-fold reason (*apologetic* and *evangelistic*) as to why he wrote his Gospel: **"But these have been written so that you may believe that Jesus is the Christ, the Son of God [*apologetic*], and that believing you may have life in His name [*evangelistic*]."**

Thus, we as Christians are called to always be ready to provide a biblical defense and a reason for our faith. The church of Ephesus was commended by Christ Himself for engaging in continuous apologetics—namely, in actively testing and finding false teachings and teachers: [2] "I know your deeds and your toil and perseverance.... [3] and you have perseverance and have endured for My name's sake, and have not grown weary" (Rev. 2:2-3).

Two

The Foundation of the Christian Faith

> *Be diligent to present yourself approved to God as a worker who does not need to be ashamed, accurately handling the word of truth (2 Tim. 2:15).*

In Romans 1:16, the Apostle Paul clearly states that the gospel "is the power of God for salvation." Hence, the "gospel" is the normal means that God uses to save His people bringing them securely to Christ. Yet, Paul declares in verse 15: "I am eager to preach the gospel [*euaggelizō*] to you also who are in Rome." Consider that Paul stated this to the Christians in Rome and not to unbelievers. So why would Paul be eager to preach the gospel (i.e., evangelize) to those who were already saved? The answer is expressed in several passages in the NT, which deal with the importance of soundness and accuracy in the proclamation of the gospel (or for that matter, any other biblical doctrine; see Eph. 4:14; 1 Tim. 4:16; 2 Tim. 2:15; Titus 2:13; 1 John 4:1-3). Thus, Paul was eager to teach and preach to the Christians in Rome a more accurate and deeper understanding of the gospel. Apologetics and evangelism start with having a set-foundation and a clear accurate understanding of the essential doctrines of the Christian faith. Without a set-foundation, biblical error is inevitable.

Today, far too many Christians, although having sufficient knowledge of Christ and the gospel, due to a lethargic attitude toward biblical study, they hold to a wide range of incomplete and/or erroneous doctrines. The fact is, all pastors/teachers should be "eager," as Paul was, to engage in higher biblical education and training based on the exegesis[1] of Scripture. In Christian schools and seminaries, higher Christian education will affect a student's life long after he or she leaves school. Unlike many secular colleges and universities, the Christian student places more worth on Christian higher education because it involves a higher learning and deeper understanding of the Redeemer, the Author of the Christian religion—Jesus Christ, "The only Sovereign and Lord" (Jude 1:4). Growing beyond a cursory level in biblical truth and knowledge of God produces a closer intimacy with the Lord and a more effectual presentation of the Christian faith (especially the gospel).

ESSENTIAL & SECONDARY THEOLOGY

Essential theology has to do with doctrines that are crucial to one's faith as a Christian. They are doctrines that have to do with Jesus' nature and finished work. For example, since the mission and work of Jesus Christ was to save sinners, essential doctrine would naturally include a literal account of Adam and Eve and thus, sin entering into the world. If the Genesis account were not a literal historic event, then; the entire effects of Adam's sin being imputed to all men would be false, a mythological invention, or a mere figurative analogy.

This, to be sure, would make the testimony of the apostles and Christ Himself erroneous since they taught that these events in Genesis and the persons involved (including the serpent) were literal events that actually happened.

---

1   Exegesis (from the Greek preposition *ex*, "out" and *hēgeomai*, "to lead") is practice of "leading out" the biblical author's intended meaning. This should be the task of all Christians—to exegete Scripture, that is, to "lead out" of the text— the author's intended God breathed meaning. Contra exegesis is eisegesis. Note the prefix of eisegesis, *eis*, "into"—thus, to "lead into." We are never to engage in *eis*egesis, that is, to "read into" the text of Scripture our own meanings. This, is what non-Christian cults and world religions habitually do.

THE GOSPEL OF THE SON

Biblically speaking, the gospel (good news) is the substitutionary and sacrificial work of Christ—not the work of man in his response, faith, repentance, good behavior, etc. Besides passages such as 1 Corinthians 15:3-4, which we will deal with shortly, Paul makes this point clear in Romans 1:1, 3: "The gospel of God.... concerning His Son." Therefore, in Paul's theology, the gospel in and of itself, has nothing to do with mere man, but everything to do with the atoning work of Jesus Christ, God the Son. We must not confuse the *work of Christ*, which is the gospel—the good news of Jesus' cross work—with the *response* of faith in Christ, repentance, obedience, etc. Salvation is *solus Christus* (through Christ alone); His work being the very ground or cause of justification and faith being the very alone instrument. The gospel then is comprised of the essential theology of the Christian faith since it involves the person, nature, and finished work of Christ. It is the atoning work of God the Son, in incarnation, death, and resurrection

In expanded detail, the essential doctrines of the Christian faith include:

- **The person of the Son is truly God and truly man, the two natured person**—being distinct from the Father who sent Him (John 1:1,[2] 14, 18; 5:17-18; 20:28; 1 Cor. 2:8; Rom. 9:5; Phil. 2:6-8; Col. 2:9; Heb. 1:3; 1 John 4:2-3; 5:20; Rev. 1:7-8).
- **The sending of the Son to earth *from* the Father–out of heaven** (John 3:13, 16-18; 6:38; 16:28).
- **Jesus being a literal *descendant* of David, born of a virgin** (2 Tim. 2:8[3]; Matt. 1:18; Rom. 9:5; Gal. 4:4; Phil. 2:6-11).
- **The perpetual (ongoing, permanent) incarnation of the Son—the Word became flesh** (John 1:1, 14; *2 Tim. 2:8*; 1 John 4:2-3; 2 John 1:7).
- **The Son's substitutionary (vicarious) atoning sinless life (preceptive obedience) and cross work (penal obedience) as the very *ground* of justification,** which removed the sin-guilt and God's wrath due to us for our sins (Gen. 15:6; Isa.

---

2 See Appendix B for a brief presentation of John 1:1.
3 "Remember Jesus Christ, risen from the dead, descendant [*spermatos*] of David, according to my gospel."

53:11; Mark 10:45; John 6:37-39; Rom. 5:6, 8, esp. v. 10; 8:32; 1 John 2:2, 4:10).

- **Salvation (justification), then, is through *faith alone* "apart from works"**; and by grace alone, through the atoning work of Christ alone (Acts 10:36, 43; Rom. 4:4-8; 5:1; Eph. 2:8-9; 2 Thess. 2:13; 2 Tim. 1:9).
- **Jesus' real death and physical resurrection** (John 2:19-21; 19:30; Acts 1:11; 17:31; Rom. 10:9; 1 Cor. 15:3-4; Titus 2:13).
- **His ascension to the Father** (John 6:62; 16:10, 28; 20:17; Acts 1:10-11; Heb. 10:12-13).
- **His (physical) second coming** (Acts 1:10-11; Titus 2:13-14; 1 John 2:28).
- **The concept of the Trinity**—namely, one true eternal God revealed in three distinct persons (see chap. 3 above).

The person of Christ (as unipersonal, i.e., distinct from the Father, and Holy Spirit), His nature (truly God truly man), and finished completed work (justification through faith alone) are necessary and indispensable to the Christian faith. They also imply other important doctrines such as "total inability," that is, in man's unconverted spiritual state he cannot (no ability) please or come to Christ (John 6:44; 8:43-44, 47; Rom. 3:10-18) due to the inherent sin-guilt (imputed sin) of all men resulting from the first sin in the Garden. These doctrines constitute the key ultimate test that distinguishes genuine Christianity from false non-Christian (atheistic) religious cults and world religions.

All must be affirmed in a basic sense, and none can be denied. Further, one cannot affirm some of these, but not the others. For example, Roman Catholicism (as discussed below) officially embraces the Trinity, deity of Christ, the incarnation, virgin birth, and Jesus' resurrection. However, because Roman Catholic doctrine rejects that the work of Christ alone is the absolute and sufficient means and ground of justification, Rome falls outside of Christian orthodoxy (cf. Gal. 1:6, 8)—hence, non-Christian. Thus, it is not the Jesus of biblical revelation that Rome embraces, rather a different Jesus and a "different gospel." Therefore, all things pertaining to the gospel are "essential" theology.

Whereas secondary theology is any doctrine that is not essential to one's salvation—namely, any doctrine that does not fundamentally deny or distort the nature and/or finished work of Christ (e.g., the OT Law, spiritual, gifts, method of water baptism, eschatology [i.e., end-time teachings], etc.). Again, the sufficiency of the gospel is the work of the Christ.

WHAT IS THE GOSPEL?

The noun "gospel" is from the Greek term *euaggelion* compound word from *eu*, "good, well" and *aggelos,* "announcement, herald, messenger, news." Thus, good news or good proclamation, "to bring good news, to announce glad tidings" (Thayer). It is normally connected with the kingdom of God and/or Christ and His atoning work. The verb, *euaggelizō* denotes the act of preaching, proclaiming, or heralding the good news.[4] Literally, in its participle form, "Gospelizing that announces the atoning work of the Son! (i.e., to gospelize! Rom. 10:15). Thus, the proclamation of the gospel is the ordinary means that God uses to save His people. Many times, the present participle form of *euaggelizō* is used, literally, "gospelizing" (or evangelizing) as in Acts 5:42: "And every day, in the temple and from house to house, they kept right on teaching and preaching Jesus as the Christ." In Acts 10:36, Peter stated: "The word which He sent to the sons of Israel, gospelizing [preaching] peace through Jesus Christ ("He is Lord of all)" (cf. also 10:36, 43).

In 1 Corinthians 15:3-4, Paul provides a summary of the gospel:

> [3] **For I delivered to you as of first importance what I also received, that Christ died for our sins according to the Scriptures,** [4] **and that He was buried, and that He was raised on the third day according to the Scriptures.**

As seen above, the incarnation of God the Son is a part of Paul's gospel—2 Tim. 2:8). Here Paul defines his simple gospel:

1. **"Christ"**

---

4 The verb appears in the LXX twenty times.

2. "Died"
3. "For our sins" and
4. "Raised on the third day"

"**Christ**"—which Christ? The Christ of Paul's gospel was *truly God* (1 Cor. 2:8; Phil. 2:6-11; Col. 2:9; Titus 2:13; 2 Pet. 1:1); born of a virgin (Gal. 4:4); and *truly man,* God incarnate (Rom. 9:5; 1 Cor. 2:8; Gal. 4:4; Col. 2:9; 1 Tim. 2:5; 2 Tim. 2:8); the Second Person of the Trinity (2 Cor. 13:14; Eph. 2:18).

"**Died**" ("for our sins"). Christ died a real death that produced a real vicarious sacrifice (Rom. 5:6, 8, 10; 8:32-33; 1 Cor. 15:3-4; Eph. 1:7; Col. 1:14).

"**For our sins.**" This phrase includes (as seen above) the Son's substitutionary atoning sacrifice (the ground of justification, i.e., being *declared* righteous/just in the sight of the Lord through faith alone, apart from works; Rom. 4:4-8; 5:1, 8-10; 8:32-33; Gal. 1:4; Eph. 2:8-9; 5:25; Col. 1:20, 22).

"**Raised on the third day.**" It was a physical resurrection (Acts 17:31; 1 Cor. 15:3-4).

Again, the gospel has to do with the Son, not the man (Rom. 1:1-3)—Jesus' work both in His perfect life (Rom. 5:10) and His death. We need a set-foundation, that is, we need to be "set" in our theology on the foundational/essential truths of the Christian faith—i.e., the gospel of the Son.

THE GOSPEL TODAY HAS THE SAME EFFICACY AND POWER AS IT DID IN THE FIRST CENTURY

As we saw in Romans 1:16, believers are saved by God alone through the preaching of the gospel. The feet of those who proclaim the gospel ("gospelizing"[5]) are "beautiful" according to the Lord (Rom. 10:15). Unfortunately, well-meaning Christian's mis-define the gospel.

---

5   Romans 10:15 reads: "And how are they to preach unless they are sent? As it is written, 'How beautiful are the feet of those who preach the good news!'" (ESV). This citation is from the LXX of Isaiah 52:7, which is the first occurrence of the verd *euaggelizō* (from *euaggelion,* "gospel"). A few interesting things to consider. First, the term translated "beautiful" is from the Greek adjective *hōraios,* which is from *hora* ("hour, time") carrying the meaning of the time when fruit comes into season, ripe. In this sense, timely, thus, beautiful. Thus, literally, "How timely is the arrival." The NET renders this portion as, "How timely is the arrival of those who proclaim the good news." Louw and Nida define the adjective as "happening at the right time" as does BDAG. Greek grammarian Bill Mounce sees the term as meaning, "ʳasonable; in prime, blooming"—or "beautiful" (as in Matt. 23:27; Acts 3:2, 10; Mounce's *Complete ʳory Dictionary of Old and New Testament Words* [Grand Rapids, MI: Zondervan Academic,

Either it is reduced to some kind of end-time assertion or, even worse, it is equated to (or results in) financial prosperity and/or some kind of "sign gift" of the Holy Spirit. Some even see the gospel as man's own work in his repentance and obedience. But as seen, none of these definitions are consistent with the biblical definition. Again, the gospel is simply the work of God the Son, Jesus Christ in His life, sacrificial death, and bodily resurrection. To say again, having a set-foundation is simply having a clear accurate understanding of the essential doctrines of the Christian faith especially pertaining to the gospel.

2006], 1246). Second, as seen above, the phrase "to preach [or 'proclaim'] the good news" is from the verb, *euaggelizomenōn,* which is the present participle of the verb *euaggelizō,* literally, "gospelizing." Accordingly, a literal rendering of this latter part of the passage would be: "Just as it is written, 'How timely [are] the feet of those gospelizing (the) good things.'"

THREE

A Concise Look at the Doctrine
of the Trinity

"Go, therefore, and make disciples of all the nations, baptizing them in the name of the Father and the Son and the Holy Spirit" (Matt. 28:19).

Essential Doctrine vs. Peripheral Doctrine. The Trinity is the very foundation of the gospel. The Trinity is the mutual operation of the Three persons that infallibly accomplishes the work of salvation, as only the triune God saves. The Trinity is the very hallmark of the Christian faith, the essential of essentials. Yet it is the most neglected doctrine in far too many Christian churches. For example, out of ignorance of the doctrine, many Christians explain it in a Oneness Pentecostal (Modalism) way (i.e., Jesus as the Father), or in an LDS (Mormon) way (i.e., separate gods). It is no great surprise that the Trinity is one of the most attacked, misrepresented, and distorted Christian doctrines, mainly by the unitarians. All religious groups that are "unitarian"[1] or unipersonal in their theology (i.e., seeing God as one person) reject the biblical doctrine of the Trinity chiefly on the basis of their false notion as to what the doctrine actually teaches. As with main unitarian or unipersonal believing religious groups such as JWs (Jehovah's Witnesses), Oneness Pentecostals, Muslims, Jews, etc. they see the Trinity as teaching three separate Gods.

Thus, because of their misrepresentation of the doctrine believing God to be unipersonal, that is, existing as one person, they naturally reject the deity of Jesus Christ falsely concluding if Jesus were God, then, there would be more than one God. Most of these groups, therefore, do not actually condemn the doctrine of the Trinity, but rather they argue against tritheism (three Gods). But this is a strawman argument that distorts and misrepresents the doctrine of the Trinity. Trinitarianism teaches that there is one eternal God revealed in three *distinct* coequal coeternal coexistent persons. Therefore, we need to show unitarians groups that the belief that the Trinity equals the belief in three Gods is a false claim that misrepresents the Trinity. In doing so; Christian-unitarian dialogue can progress a lot further. Yet nowhere does the Bible teach that God is one person, rather He is one Being revealed in three distinct persons. All the passages that speak of God alone or as one, simply mean God exists as one Being, not one person. The very foundation of the doctrine of the Trinity is monotheism—namely, one true God by nature (Deut. 6:4; 32:39; Jer. 10:10-11; Mark 12:29-30; 1 Tim. 2:5).

TRINITY: *One God revealed in three coequal coeternal coexistent distinct persons.* **Or,** *there are three divine persons that share the nature of the one Being.*

Useful Notes:

All analogies of the Trinity are deficient. Most communicate either a Oneness-modalistic concept (esp. when using the "ice" analogy) or a polytheistic concept (separate gods). Instead, the biblical evidence should be used as outlined below. Historically, the concept of the Trinity was clearly taught in the early church, by both Eastern and Western church Fathers. "The plural 'We' was regarded by the

---

1   A distinction, though, needs to be made between religious groups that are unitarian in their doctrine of God and the official Unitarian religion itself. The former would include such religious systems as Judaism, Islam, Oneness Pentecostals, JWs, etc., while the latter is applied exclusively to the Unitarian Church. Thus, "unitarian" refers to the unipersonal theology of the vast number of unitarian groups. Hence, a unitarian belief of God is synonymous with a unipersonal belief of God.

fathers and earlier theologians almost unanimously as indicative of the Trinity" (Keil & Delitzsch, Genesis 1:26, Vol. 1, Page 38). Patristic authority, J. N. D. Kelly states:

> The reader should notice how deeply the conception of a plurality of divine Persons was imprinted in the apostolic tradition and the popular faith. Though as yet uncanonized, the New Testament was already exerting a powerful influence; it is a commonplace that the outlines of a dyadic and a triadic pattern are clearly visible in its pages.[2]

Examples–pre-Nicene, A.D. 325:

Didache (c. A.D. 70). "And concerning baptism, baptize this way: Having first said all these things, baptize into the name of the Father, and of the Son, and of the Holy Spirit, in living water. But if you have no living water, baptize into other water; and if you cannot do so in cold water, do so in warm. But if you have neither, pour out water three times upon the head into the name of Father and Son and Holy Spirit" (Chap. 7).[3]

Ignatius of Antioch (A.D. 107). In Ignatius's genuine letters, Ignatius frequently refers to Christ as *ho Theos* ("the God") or a similar phrase, and does so in grammatical distinction from the Father (Romans-prologue; Eph. 18; Polycarp 8.3 et al.). In his *Letter to the Romans,* Ignatius states: "For our God, Jesus Christ, now that He is with the Father, is all the more revealed [in His glory]...." (3).

In his *Letter to the Magnesians* 6:1, Ignatius affirms the eternal pre-existence of Jesus *being with* the Father: "Jesus Christ, who *before the ages* [*pro aiōnōn*] was *with the Father* [*para Patri*] and appeared at the end of time...."[4] (emphasis added).

---

2 J. N. D. Kelly, *Early Christian Doctrines* (San Francisco, CA: HarperCollins, 1978), 88.
3 Roberts & Donaldson (eds.), *Ante-Nicene Fathers* (Peabody, MA: Hendrickson, 1994).
4 Note the linguistic parallel between John 17:5 ("And now You, Father, glorify Me together with Yourself, with the glory which I had with You before the world existed") and *Magnesians* 6:1 ("Jesus Christ, who before the ages was with the Father...."). Ignatius uses the same verb tenses (*imperfect*), same prepositional phrase (*para* + dative), and the same preposition (*pro*) as in John 17:5 to denote the eternal preexistence of the person of the Son being *with* the Father. First, both John and Ignatius use imperfect verbs to indicate the *past ongoing* preexistence of the Son: **John 17:5**: "with the glory,

Justin Martyr (A.D. 160). Justin cites the Trinitarian formula in Matthew 28:19 in *The First Apology*, 61.1. In *Dialogue with Trypho the Jew*, 62, Justin refers to Genesis 1:26 emphasizing the Hebrew plural verb ("let Us make") seeing the preincarnate Christ included in the "Us" who created man, being "numerically distinct from the Father":

"Let Us make," –I shall quote again the words narrated by Moses himself, from which we can indisputably learn that [God] conversed with someone who *was numerically distinct [kai arithmō heteron]* from Himself, and also a rational Being (emphasis added).

In the same work (*Dialogue with Trypho*), Justin refers to Genesis 19:24 ("YHWH rained brimstone and fire from YHWH out from heaven"], in which Justin declares: "And that Christ being Lord, and God the Son of God, and appearing formerly in power as Man, and Angel, and in the glory of fire as at the bush, so also was manifested at the judgment executed on Sodom."

Clement of Alexandria (c. A.D. 190): "I understand nothing else than the Holy Trinity to be meant; for the third is the Holy Spirit, and the Son is the second, by whom all things were made according to the will of the Father" (*Stromata*, Book V, Ch. 14).

Tertullian (c. A.D. 213): "He commands them to baptize into the Father and the Son and the Holy Ghost, not into a unipersonal God. And indeed it is not once only, but three times, that we are immersed into the Three Persons, at each several mention of Their names (*Against Praxeas*, 26).

Dionysius, bishop of Alexandria (c. A.D. 262): "The Son alone, always co-existing with the Father.... Thus, indeed, we expand the indivisible Unity into a Trinity; and again we contract the Trinity, which cannot be diminished, into a Unity" ("Epistle to Dionysius Bishop of Rome," 5-9, in *Works of Dionysius, Extant Fragments*).

---

which **I had** [or 'shared,' *eichon*] with You"; *Magnesians* **6:1**: "Jesus Christ, who before the ages **was** [ēn] with the Father." In John 1:1, the same imperfect verb (*ēn*, "was") is used in John 1:1 denoting the same thing! "In the beginning **was** the Word, and the Word **was** with God, and the Word **was** God" (see, Appendix B: John 1:1 below). Second, both John and Ignatius use the same prepositional phrase, *para* ("with") with the dative case clearly indicating association and distinction between the persons of the Son and the Father: **John 17:5**: "And now You, Father, glorify Me **together with Yourself** [*para seautō*] ... with the glory, which I had **with You** [*para soi*]"; *Magnesians* **6:1**: "Jesus Christ who before the ages was **with the Father** [*para Patri*]." Third, both John and Ignatius use the same preposition *pro* ("before") indicting the actual preexistence of the person of the Son: **John 17:5**: "with the Father *before* [*pro*] the world was"; *Magnesians* **6:1**: "Jesus Christ, who **before the ages** [*pro aiōnōn*] was with the Father."

Gregory Thaumaturgus (c. A.D. 262): "But some treat the Holy Trinity in an awful manner, when they confidently assert that there are not three persons, and introduce (the idea of) a person devoid of subsistence.... we believe that three persons, namely, Father, Son, and Holy Spirit, are declared to possess the one Godhead: for the one divinity showing itself forth according to nature in the Trinity establishes the oneness of the nature" (*A Sectional Confession of Faith,* 7).

And many more pre-Nicene references could be cited, which clearly affirmed the concept of the Trinity.

THE THREE BIBLICAL TRUTHS

As seen, the Trinity could be summed up in a simple sentence such as *There is one God who is revealed in three coequal coeternal coexistent distinct persons.* However, even more descriptive is to declare the three biblical suppositions or truths of the Trinity (don't use analogies!). The following is the scriptural proof texts for each truth:

1. **There is only one true God** (Exod. 20:5; Deut. 6:4; Isa. 43:10; 45:5; *Jer. 10:10-11*; Mark 12:29-30 et al.). Not *one person* (as all unitarian groups[5] assert), rather, *one Being.*
2. **There are three persons or** *selves* **that are presented as God:** the Father,[6] the Son,[7] and the Holy Spirit.[8]
3. **The three divine persons are distinct from each other** (Gen. 19:24; Dan. 7:9-14; Matt. 28:19; John 1:1, 18; 6:38; 17:5; 2 Cor. 13:14; Eph. 2:18; 2 John 1:3; Rev. 5:13-14 et al.; see below).

Therefore, the three distinct persons share the nature or Being of the one true God.

COMMON OBJECTIONS TO THE DOCTRINE OF THE TRINITY MADE BY UNITARIANS GROUPS

The three most utilized objectives to the Trinity are

---

5 Such as Muslims, JWs, Unitarians, Oneness advocates et al., as explained above.

6 The distinct person of the Father is truly God (Luke 10:21-22; John 1:1b; 17:3; Rom. 5:10; Gal. 1:3).

7 The Son, Jesus Christ, is also unipersonal (a distinct person) and is called and presented as *Theos* ("God"), *Kurios* ("Lord") in a religious context, and presented as YHWH in both the OT and NT. He is also presented as the Creator of all things, and was worshiped in a religious context—namely, as truly God (Dan. 7:13-14; Matt. 14:27, 33; John 9:35-38; Heb. 1:6; Rev. 5:13-14).

8 The Holy Spirit also is presented as God and as a *distinct person.* See Appendix A for biblical proof texts.

1. The term "Trinity" is not found in the Bible.
2. The Trinity teaches three Gods, and
3. The Trinity was invented in the fourth century (viz. at the Council of Nicaea, A.D. 325) and thus, it is nowhere taught in the Bible (not even the term is there).

First objection. Since the word "Trinity" is not in Bible it must be a false doctrine. This argument is nonsensical for many reasons. It is true that nowhere in the Bible does the exact word Trinity appear. If the ones using this argument were consistent, then, they would not believe that God is one person either because the word "unitarian" does not appear in the Bible. In point of fact, Christians today (as well as the early Christian church, as noted above) use the *doctrinal* term Trinity to describe God because it plainly and adequately denotes the teaching and concept of a triune multi-personal God presented throughout Scripture. Consider that the terms: incarnation, coequal, coeternal (with the Father), and the phrases: *hypostatic union, God the Son, substitutionary atonement,* etc., which are all true of Christ, do not appear in the Bible. Also, the terms *omnipresent, omniscient, omnipotent, self-existent,* etc., which are all ascribed to God, do not appear in the Bible; however, the teachings or concepts of these doctrinal words and phrases do. They are clearly expressed in the biblical content.

Here are some of the doctrinal (nonbiblical) words mentioned above with their corresponding biblical passages expressing the teachings and concepts of these words:

Incarnation. This defines the teaching of God the Son becoming flesh - John 1:14 et al.

God the Son (Mark 14:61-64; John 1:1, 18; Heb. 1:8, 10; 1 John 5:20 et al.).

Hypostatic union of Jesus Christ. This describes the two natures of Christ, God and man (John1:14; 1 Cor. 2:8; Phil. 2:6-7-8; 2 Tim. 2:8).

The Son's coequality and coeternality with the Father (Gen. 19:24; John 1:1c; 5:17-18; 10:30- 33; 17:5; Heb. 1:3, 6, 8-12; Jude 1:4; Rev. 1:8, 5:13-14; 22:13).

Substitutionary atonement. This describes Jesus' atoning cross work as a literal substitution for and on behalf of the elect (John 6:37-39; 10:17; Mark 10:45; Rom. 8:32; Gal. 1:4; Eph. 5:25; 1Tim. 2:6).

Omnipresent. An attribute ascribed to God (Ps. 139:6-10; John 14:23 et al.).

Although there are many more doctrinal words that can be mentioned that are not contained in the Bible, they all do indeed express the biblical teachings and concepts they represent.

Second objection (The Trinity = 3 separate Gods.): To say that the Trinity teaches three Gods is a gross misrepresentation of the doctrine. As noted, the very foundation of the Trinity is monotheism—namely, the Bible teaches that there is only one true God. Three Gods/gods is not biblical trinitarianism rather, it is polytheism (many true Gods/ gods, or henotheism[9]), in which both the OT and NT condemn (Exod. 20:5; Isa. 43:10; 45:5; Mark 12:28-29; 1 Tim. 2:5 et al.). As shown above, the Bible teaches that there are three distinct persons who share the nature of the one true God. Or, there is one true God (one Being) who is revealed in *three coequal coeternal coexistent distinct persons*—the Father, and the Son, and the Holy Spirit. As delineated above, the three biblical propositions or truths affirm the Trinity.

1. **There is one true eternal God (viz., one Being).**
2. **There are three persons referred to as God, YHWH, and the Creator of all things— the Father, and the Son, and the Holy Spirit.**
3. **These three persons are *distinct* from each other.**

Third objection (The Trinity wasn't invented until the Council of Nicaea, A.D. 325). First, the issue at the Council of Nicaea was not the Trinity, that had already been established in the early church decades before Nicaea. In point of fact, there are no primary source documents that came out of Nicaea that even mention the term "Trinity" or specifically discuss it. Instead, the Council primarily addressed the heretical teachings of Arius who openly taught that the Son was created, "a god," but *not* "Almighty God," similar to what the JWs teach. Arius taught that Jesus was of a "*different* substance" than that of the Father in direct opposition to the orthodox position, which taught that Jesus was of the "*same* substance" (*homoousios,* viz. coequal, consubstantial) as that of the Father, but not the same person. So, the chief issue at Nicaea was the question of the ontological relationship between the

---

9   Henotheism (*hen,* "one" *theos,* "god") is the belief that although many true Gods/gods exist, worship and devotion is to only one God. Hinduism and Mormonism hold to this view. Mormons acknowledge the existence of many *true* Gods of other planets, but they only worship and the God for this planet. See discussion below on the LDS (Mormon) Church.

Father and the Son—not the Trinity *per se*. Further, details of Arius and the Council of Nicaea and its resulting Creed are discussed below."

FOUR

The Son of God

> For this reason therefore the Jews were seeking all the more to kill Him, because He not only was breaking the Sabbath, but also was calling God His own Father, making Himself equal with God (John 5:18)

"Tons of sons!"- the angry Muslim shouts out in his flimsy attempt to "refute" Christians who proclaim the deity of Christ. In other words, unitarians groups (esp. Muslims) deny that Jesus' unique claim to be the "Son of God" was in fact a claim of deity, that is, truly God. Muslims, for example, are taught that Jesus was only speaking metaphorically when He referred to Himself as the Son of God (Mark 14:61-64; John 10:30-36). Muslims, along with JWs, mistakenly assume that if Jesus is the Son of God, He cannot be God. Of course, they start with their unitarian assumption (God is one person), from which their conclusions flow. These unitarian groups also argue that Jesus was the Son of God by doing good works, glorifying God, being humble, etc., thus, He was not the "one and only" (monogenēs) Son in a unique sense. Unitarians further point out that both in the OT and NT there were many who were referred to as a "son of God" or God's son—such as Adam (Luke 3:38); Israel (Exod. 4:22); judges (Ps. 82:6); David (Ps. 89:27); Ephraim (Jer. 31:9); Jews (John 8:41); Christians (Gal. 3:26); and even angels (Gen. 6:2; Job 1:6; 38:7). So, as it is argued, if the title "Son of God" indicates deity, then Adam, David, angels, etc. are also God. In response, it must first be pointed out that the meaning of biblical words and phrases are determined by the context (as with the term Elohim).

Second, in a Semitic (Jewish) context, to be the "son of" something frequently meant that one possesses or shares the nature of that something. Ephesians 2:2-3, for example, the unsaved are said to be the "sons of disobedience ... by nature children of wrath," in that they possess the nature of disobedience and wrath. Unbelievers are said to be "sons of the Devil" (John 8:44), whereas believers are "sons of God" by adoption (Eph. 1:5), through faith (Gal. 3:26).

JESUS CHRIST, THE UNIQUE SON OF GOD

Even though the phrase "son(s) of God" was applied to angels and men, when it was applied to Jesus, it was in a context of essence or nature. Christians are sons of God by adoption, Jesus is the Son of God by nature[1]—which was clearly a claim of being God the Son. In a similar ontological semantic (as a title of absolute deity), Jesus' also identified Himself as the "Son of Man"[2] (Mark 10:45; 13:26; 14:61-62; John 1:51; 3:13; 5:27; 6:62 et al.; cf. Dan. 7:13-14).

---

1   Although, not a son in a biological sense (as LDS teaches; see below), but rather, in a relational sense.

2   Especially in light of Daniel 7:13-14, Son of Man was a well-recognized epithet. Jesus identified Himself as the Son of Man approximately eighty times in the Gospels (His preferred title of Himself). In Mark 14:61-64, when questioned as to His identity, Jesus declared to the high priest, "I am [the Messiah and the Son of God]; and you shall see the Son of Man sitting at the right hand of power, and coming with the clouds of heaven." Against the backdrop of Daniel 7:13 ("I kept looking in the night visions, and behold, with the clouds of heaven One like a son of man was coming"), the high priest clearly understood that Jesus' claim to be both the Son of God and the Son of Man as claims of absolute deity.

Consider these examples below:

John 5:17-18. Son of God, God the Son:

¹⁶ For this reason the Jews were persecuting Jesus, because He was doing these things on a Sabbath. ¹⁷ But He answered them, "My Father is working until now, and I Myself am working." ¹⁸ For this reason therefore the Jews were seeking all the more to kill Him, because He not only was breaking the Sabbath, but also was calling God His own Father, making Himself equal with God.

One of the best examples of where Jesus' claim to be the "Son of God" denoted ontological (viz. in very nature) equality with God is found in the Gospel of John chapter 5. In verse 17, Jesus said, "My Father is working until now, and I Myself am working." This was Jesus' response to the charges brought against Him. The Father's creative activity stopped after six days, but not His governing and upholding the universe. However, the Son's activity of mediating, rewarding, punishing, etc. is ongoing. Then we read in verse 18: "For this reason therefore the Jews were seeking all the more to kill Him, because He was not only breaking the Sabbath, but He was also calling God His Father, making Himself equal with God." The Jews (and the Apostle John) clearly understood that by Jesus claiming God was His Father (i.e., the Son of God), He was unambiguously claiming to be "equal with God." This is confirmed by the sharp response of the Jews, "For this reason therefore the Jews were seeking all the more to kill Him, because He was ... calling God His Father, making Himself equal with God." As a similar response is found in John 19:7, "We have a law, and by that law He ought to die because He made Himself out to be the Son of God."

As indicated, this sharply opposes the position of those who assert that Jesus' claim to be the Son of God was not a claim to be equal with God. There is one more notable feature in this text. The verbs translated, "breaking" (*eluen,* lit., "relaxing, losing") and "calling" (*elegen*) as in "calling God His Father" are both in the imperfect tense. The force of an imperfect tense indicates a continuous or repeated action normally occurring in the past. Thus, apparently, this was not the first time He made these claims—He had been repeating these claims. In addition, the *reflexive* pronoun (*heauton*, "Himself"), which grammatically indicates that the action of "making Himself equal with God" was made by and for Christ Himself: "*He Himself* was making Himself equal with God."[3] So, it was not merely the view of the Jews, rather it was Jesus Himself who made Himself equal with God the Father, as the Apostle John indicates.[4]

John 10:30. "I and the Father are one" (*Egō kia ho Patēr hen esmen*, lit., "I and the Father one we are"). Both historically and currently, Christians have pointed to this passage to show that Jesus indeed claimed equality with God the Father. As with Jesus' other undeniable claims to be truly God (Matt. 12:6; John 5:17-18; 8:58-59 et al; Rev. 1:7-8, 17; 2:8; 22:13; etc.), the response of the Jews in verse 33 hence, is an irrefutable confirmation of Jesus' claim: "For a good work we do not stone You, but for blasphemy; and because You, being a man, make Yourself out to be God." This passage also provides a clear refutation to the Oneness view (as discussed below), which erroneously asserts that Jesus *is* the Father (the same person). Ironically, Oneness advocates actually use John 10:30 as a so-called proof text, aside from the fact that throughout chapter 10, Jesus and the Father are clearly differentiated as two persons (vv. 15, 17, 18, 25, 29, 30, 36, 37, 38). However, the following points regarding John 10:30 clearly refute Oneness theology:

Not one person within conservative recognized Christian scholarship agrees with a Oneness interpretation. Neither historically nor contemporaneously has any Christian writer interpreted John 10:30 in a modalistic (Oneness) way. Rather, all standard scholarly sources (patristics, commentaries, grammars, lexicons et al), interpret the passage in the plain intended way, within the defining context:

---

3   The reflexive pronoun is where the subject is also the object of the action of the verb. It intensifies the identification of the subject as participating in the action of the verb. "On a broader scale, the reflexive pronoun is used to *highlight the participation of the subject* in the verbal action, as a direct object, indirect object, intensifier, etc." (Daniel Wallace, *Greek Grammar Beyond the Basics* [GGBB]: *An Exegetical Syntax of the New Testament, with Scripture, Subject, and Greek Word Indexes* [Grand Rapids, MI: Zondervan, 1996], 350). Paul uses the reflexive pronoun in Philippians 2:7 and verse 8 to indicate that the *emptying* and *humbling* of Jesus was something that Jesus, God the Son Himself did by and for Himself. Consequently, it was self-emptying and self-humbling.

4   See discussion on the reflexive pronoun in John 10:33 below.

The person of the Son claiming equality with the distinct person of the Father.

Plain reading. Jesus simply says, "I and the Father ARE one." Only by pretexting can one read something into this text beyond the simple plain reading.

The neuter adjective *hen* ("one") is used—contextually indicating a unity of essence, not personal identity. If Jesus wanted to identify Himself as the same person as the Father, He certainly could have used the masculine *heis* to indicate this (e.g., John 12:4; Rom. 3:10; 1 Tim. 2:5 et al.). In this passage, the Father and the Son are the two subjects of the sentence (*egō*, "I," and *Patēr*, "Father"—both in the nominative [subject] case). The neuter adjective *hen* ("one") is the predicate nominative and it precedes the plural verb *esmen* ("are").

The predicate nominative "one" is describing the essential unity of the two subjects, Jesus and the Father.[5] In other words, Jesus is explaining that the Father and Son are *one in essence,* not one person, in the context of unity, not identity of person. The same neuter adjective is used in John 17:21, expressing unity (not person) where Jesus prays that His disciples "may be one [*hen*]" even as Jesus and the Father are one. However, in verse 30, it was a unity in ontological coequality that Jesus expressed—thus, "The Jews picked up stones again to stone Him" (v. 31).

The plural verb *esmen* ("are"). Again, in sharp contrast to the false Oneness interpretation (viz., that *Jesus is the Father*), the Greek contains the plural verb *esmen* ("I and the Father are one"), and not a singular verb such as *eimi* ("am") or *estin* ("is") in which case, the passage would read: "I and the Father am/is one." Furthermore, Jesus' claim to deity is not merely found in verse 30. But rather, the passages leading up to verse 30 undeniably prove His claim. In verses 27-29, Jesus claims that He is the Shepherd that gives His sheep eternal life and no one can snatch them from His nor His Father's hand (same words of YHWH in the LXX of Deut. 32:39[6]). The Jews were well

---

5   Renowned Greek grammarian A. T. Robertson comments on the application of the neuter *hen* in John 10:30: "One (*hen*). Neuter, not masculine (*heis*). Not one person (cf. *heis* in Gal. 3:28), but one essence or nature" (Archibald T. Robertson, *Word Pictures in the New Testament* [Nashville, TN: Broadman Press, 1932], 5:186).

6   **Deuteronomy 32:39** (LXX): "And there is no one who can deliver *ek tōn cheirōn Mou*" ("out of the hands of Me"). **John 10:28**: "they will never perish; and no one will snatch them *ek tēs cheiros Mou*" ("out of the hand of Me"). **John 10:29**: "no one is able to snatch them *ek tēs cheiros tou Patros*" ("out of the hand of the Father").

acquainted with Deuteronomy 32:39: "And there is no one who can save anyone from My hand" and Psalm 95:7: "For He is our God, and we are the people of His pasture and the sheep of His hand." The Jews knew that only YHWH could make these claims of having sheep in His hand and giving them eternal life (cf. also Isa. 43:11). It was after Jesus made these familiar and exclusively divine claims that He stated, "I and the Father are one."

Not mere unity, rather, unity in ontological coequality. So, it is easy to understand the response of the Jews wanting to kill Him for blasphemy: "You, being a man, **make Yourself out to be God** [*poieis seauton Theon*]" (vv. 31, 33).[7] If Jesus were only claiming to be "one" with the Father in the sense of mere unity, then Jesus' claim would not have warranted blasphemy (Lev. 24:16).

THE SON WAS IDENTIFIED AS YHWH

I. Angel of the LORD

Many places in the NT identify Jesus, the Son of God, as YHWH: "[Jesus answered] your father Abraham was overjoyed that he would see My day, and he saw it and rejoiced" (Jn. 8:56). One such reference is the OT character of the "angel of the LORD/God. In both Hebrew and Greek, the term "angel" simply means "messenger" (Heb. *malak*, Greek, *aggelos*). Only context determines if the *malak/aggelos*, thus, "messenger" is a human prophet (Isa. 42:19; 44:26), a priest (Mal. 2:7), a heavenly angel sent from God, or, the preincarnate divine Son. In the OT, this unique "angel of the LORD" claimed to be YHWH (Exod. 3:6, 14); and the one who encountered Him identified Him as YHWH/God for example,

- **Hagar** (Gen. 16:7-13). In verse 13, Hagar said to Him: "You are a God who sees all." The LXX reads: *Su ho Theos epidōn me,* "**You are the God**, the one seeing me."
- **Abraham** (Gen. chaps. 18-19, esp. 19:24; cf. 22:11-19).
- **Moses** (Exod. 3:1-6, 14). In verse 6, the angel of the LORD declared to Moses: "I am the God of your father, the God of

---

7   As in John 5:18, in John 10:33, the second person reflexive pronoun *seauton* ("Yourself") indicates that the Jews understood that Jesus' claims in John 10, which culminated in verse 30 ("I and the Father are one") were by and for Himself—namely, He Himself made Himself "out to be God."

Abraham, the God of Isaac, and the God of Jacob." And in 3:14, He stated (LXX): *egō eimi ho ōn,* literally, "I am the One timelessly existing (viz., the eternal One).[8]

- **Balaam** (Num. 22:22-35).
- **Gideon** (Judg. 6:11-24).
- **Manoah** (Judg. 13:3-21; esp. vv. 5-7, 16, 23).

There are many more references of the angel of the LORD (cf. Josh. 5:13-15;[9] 2 Kings 19:35 et al.). However, the examples mentioned above are more than sufficient in showing that the angel of the LORD was identified as YHWH Himself, the person of the preincarnate Christ, and yet distinct from another YHWH (esp. Gen. 19:24; Zech. 1:12[10] et al.), which is consistent with the doctrine of the Trinity. We find the same in the NT, personal interaction with the Son and the Father (Luke 10:21-22; John 17:5; 14:23; Heb. 1:8-12). Also, these angel of the LORD references of the preincarnate Son were speaking of the Son in actual preexistence, not merely in prophecy. Even more, these OT references reveal the personal interaction of the preincarnate divine Son with others. It is not a difficult task to discover that Jesus was indeed identified as YHWH, and not merely a representative or agent of YHWH.

---

8   As mentioned below, the articular ("the") participial phrase (or adjectival participle), *ho ōn* ("the one who is"), carries the denotative meaning of "timeless existence," or eternality when applied to Christ (viz. at John 1:18; 6:46; Rom. 9:5; and Rev. 1:8). John 1:18 reads, "No one has seen God at any time; the one and only God [or 'Son' in later MSS] **who is** [*ho ōn,* i.e., 'the One who is/being always'] in the bosom of the Father, He has explained Him" (emphasis added); Romans 9:5, "Whose are the fathers, and from whom is the Christ according to the flesh, **who is** [*ho ōn,* i.e., 'the One who is/being always'] over all, God blessed forever. Amen" (emphasis added); Revelation 1:8 (in light of v. 7), "'I am the Alpha and the Omega,' says the Lord God, '**who is** [*ho ōn,* i.e., "the One who is/being always"] and who was and who is to come, the Almighty'" (emphasis added). So, in Exodus 3:14, the angel of the LORD (preincarnate Son) stated His identity to Moses: *egō eimi ho ōn*— "I am the One timelessly existing, the eternal One." Regarding the article participle (*ho ōn*) in John 1:18, NT scholar Murry Harris explains that it "denotes the Son's eternal existence" (Murray J. Harris, *Jesus as God: The New Testament Usage of Theos in Reference to Jesus* [Grand Rapids, MI: Baker, 1992], 57-58).

9   Especially notice verses 14-15: 14 "[Joshua] said, 'No; rather I indeed come now as captain of the host of the LORD.' And Joshua fell on his face to the earth, and bowed down, and said to Him, 'What has my lord to say to his servant?' 15 The captain of the LORD'S host said to Joshua, 'Remove your sandals from your feet, for the place where you are standing is holy.' And Joshua did so." This is exactly what the angel of the LORD said to Moses in Exodus 3:5: "Remove your sandals from your feet, for the place on which you are standing is holy ground." Nowhere in Scripture is it even implied that being in the presence of mere angels is "holy ground" in which one must remove his sandals. John the Baptist speaks of the coming Christ before whom he is "not fit to remove His sandals" (Matt. 3:11). Thus, John saw the presence of the Christ, as God incarnate, sacred.

10   In this passage, we see the angel of the LORD, who from Genesis onwards, has been identified as YHWH, now here praying to YHWH.

II. OT passages referring to YHWH that are applied to the Son in the NT.

Aside from the angel of the LORD references, the NT authors frequently cited specific OT passages explicitly referring to YHWH and/or His activities and applied them explicitly to the preincarnate Son. For example:

Psalm 102:25-27 with Hebrews 1:10-12: The Father addresses the Son as the Lord—namely, the YHWH of Psalm 102:25-27, the unchangeable Creator of all things (Heb. 1:10-12 will be treated in detail below).

Isaiah 6:1-10 with John 12:39-41: In John 12:39-40, John cites the prophecy of Isaiah 6:10 (LXX) to explain why the Jews were not believing in Jesus. Note the LXX of Isaiah 6:1, 3: [1] *"eidon ton Kurion* ['I saw the Lord'] ... and the house was full *tēs doxēs autou* ['of the glory of Him']. [3] ... "Holy, Holy, Holy, is the Lord of armies: the whole earth is full *tēs doxēs autou* ["of the glory of Him']"—referring to YHWH. In John 12:40, John cites the LXX of Isaiah 6:10. But note John 12:41, John uses the same Greek base verbs and phrases as in the LXX of Isaiah 6:1, 3: "These things [i.e., Isa. 6:1-10] Isaiah said because *eiden* ['he saw'] *tēn doxan autou* ['the glory of Him'] and he spoke about Him [Christ]." Hence, according to John, the YHWH on the throne that Isaiah saw and spoke about, and around which the seraphim were flying, was the preincarnate Son, Christ Jesus.

Isaiah 8:12-13 with 1 Peter 3:14-15. As discussed above, in Peter 3:14-15 (CT reading)[11], Peter cites the LXX of Isaiah 8:12-13, which in verse 13, YHWH told Isaiah that they must "sanctify the LORD Himself" (LXX, *Kurion* [Heb. YHWH] *auton hagiasate*, "[the] LORD Himself sanctify"). To recall,[12] both the LXX of Isaiah and Peter in 1 Peter 3:15, use the same verb *hagiasate* ("to sanctify") in the same tense and mood—aorist imperative. Again, Peter identifies Jesus Christ as the YHWH of Isaiah 8:13 that should be sanctified.

Isaiah 45:23 with Philippians 2:10-11. In Isaiah 45:23, YHWH says that "Surely every knee will bend to Me, every tongue will solemnly confess." Yet, in Philippians 2:10-11, the Apostle Paul (drawing from the LXX), identifies Jesus Christ as the YHWH of the future

---

11 Cf note 1 above.
12 Cf. note 2 above.

prophecy of Isaiah 45:23: Before whom every knee shall bend and every tongue shall confess (see below for discussion on Phil. 2:6-11).
Joel 2:32 with Romans 10:13. In Romans 10:9, Paul says "That if you confess with your mouth **Jesus as Lord**, and believe in your heart that God raised **Him** [Jesus] from the dead, you will be saved." Grammatically, the antecedent to the pronoun (**"Him"**) in verses 9 and 11 and the **"Lord"** in verses 9 and 12 refer back to the closest named person, which we find in verse 9: "Jesus as Lord." Thus, keeping grammatically consistent, the "Lord" in verse 13 also refers back to Jesus. And notice there is no switch of persons or a different Lord mentioned from verses 9-13, it is the person of Christ Jesus who is Lord. However, in verse 13, Paul cites Joel 2:32: "Everyone who calls on the name of the LORD [Heb. YHWH] will be saved." According to Paul, then, the YHWH that one must confess for salvation is Jesus Christ, the Son of God. Verses 9 and 13 say fundamentally mean the same thing: one must confess Jesus Christ as Lord [viz. YHWH] for salvation. The Apostle Paul along with John,[13] Peter,[14] James,[15] Jude,[16] God the Father,[17] and Christ Jesus Himself,[18] identify Christ the Son as YHWH. He is the YHWH of Joel 2:32, and the YHWH and fulfillment of Isaiah 45:23—*before whom every knee shall bend and every*

---

13 John 12:41; Revelation 1:8, 17; 2:8; 22:13.

14 1 Peter 3:15; 2 Peter 1:1.

15 James 2:1. The NASB reads: "My brothers and sisters, do not hold your faith in our glorious Lord Jesus Christ with an attitude of personal favoritism." The Greek phrase from which the translation, the "our glorious Lord Jesus Christ" is *tou kuriou hēmōn Iēsou Christou tēs doxēs*, lit., "of the Lord of us Jesus Christ of glory." Most translations have "glorious Lord Jesus Christ" (NASB, NET et al.) seeing *doxēs* as an attributive genitive (adjectival force), that is, describing an attribute or quality to the head noun, which here is Jesus Christ. However, many others translate the phrase as, "Lord Jesus Christ, the Lord of glory" (KJV, ESV et al.). Although the Greek has been subject to many discussions among commentators, in 1 Corinthians 2:8, the Apostle Paul referred to Christ as "the Lord of glory." Further, similar titles to "the Lord of glory" were used of YHWH alone (1 Sam. 15:29 ["the Glory of Israel"]; Acts 7:2 ["the God of glory"]). Also, in Ephesians 1:17, the Father is referred to as "the Father of glory." In fact, all these titles are from the same genitive phrase as in James 2:1: *Iēsou Christou tēs doxēs,* "Jesus Christ of the glory."
   Ephesians 1:17: *Ho Patēr tēs doxēs,* "the Father of the glory."
   Acts 7:2: *Ho Theos tēs doxēs,* "the God of the glory."
   1 Corinthians 2:8: *Ton Kurion tēs doxēs,* "The Lord of the glory."

16 John 1:4-5.

17 Hebrews 1:10-12 (esp. 1:6).

18 E.g., Matthew 12:6, 8; Mark 14:61-64; John 5:17-18; the *egō eimi* ("I am") claims (Matt. 14:27; Mark 6:50; John 8:24, 28, 58; 13:19; 18:5, 6, 8); the "First and Last" claims (Rev. 1:17; 2:8; 22:13); the "Alpha and Omega" claims (Rev. 1:8; 22:13).

tongue shall confess: Jesus Christ is YHWH to the glory of God the Father.[19]

III. The Son was Worshiped in a Religious Context

In the few samples below, the object of the verbal action of "worship" (*proskuneō*) is the Son. In each case, the surrounding context indicates that the worship was in a religious context,[20] that is, divine worship:

Daniel 7:14: "And to Him was given dominion, glory and a kingdom, that all the peoples, nations and men of every language might SERVE Him. His dominion is an everlasting dominion, which will not pass away; and His kingdom is one, which will not be destroyed." The term "serve" (NASB et al. or "worshiped" as in the NIV) is from the Aramaic imperfect verb, *pelach* (Heb. *palach*). When this term appears in the OT where God *is the object*, it carries the idea of religious worship, services, or rituals performed in honor of and directed to the true God. The same term (*pelach*) applied to the Son of Man in verse 14 is applied to YHWH in verse 27: "His kingdom will be an everlasting kingdom, and all the dominions will **serve** [*pelach*] and obey Him."

Further, the LXX (Swete and Rahlfs eds.) reads: "all glory to Him [Son of Man] **worshiping**." The Greek verb translated "worshiping" is *latreuousa,* which is the present active participle of *latreuō*. The Greek base verb *latreuō,* which, in a religious context, denotes service or worship *reserved for God alone* (cf. Exod. 20:5 [LXX]; see also Matt. 4:10; Rom. 1:9; Phil. 3:3; Heb. 9:14).

Matthew 14:33: "And those who were in the boat worshiped [*proskuneō*][21] **Him, saying, 'You are certainly God's Son!'"** The worship to the Son was in a religious context, thus, they worshiped the Son as God. First, they worshiped the Son and "kept saying"[22]

---

19 Paul in others places identifies Christ as YHWH (e.g., 1 Cor. 2:8; Titus 2:13 et al.) as does James in 2:1. And of course, as we clearly saw above, Jesus claims Himself to be YHWH. The NT authors also identified the Holy Spirit as YHWH (Acts 5:9; 28:25-27, Heb. 3:7; 10:15).

20 A religious context is any such context where holiness, reverence, devotion, godliness, divinity, etc. are in view. Such as the kind or quality of worship given to the Son by all the angels in Hebrews 1:6—for the setting is in heaven—a pure religious context.

21 The Greek word *proskuneō* means divine worship in a religious context (as with Matt. 4:10 and John 4:24) or it can also mean to fall prostrate in front of another in honor and respect, thus, "obeisance." Only the context determines the meaning. In Hebrews 1:6, as mentioned, the setting is in the heavenlies—hence, the Father urgently commands "all the angels" to give religious worship to the divine Son.

22 The verb translated "saying" is a present active participle (*legontes*), indicating that the men in the boat "kept saying" (ongoing) that Christ was the Son of God.

to Him, "You are the Son of God," which was semantically equiva-lent to saying He was God the Son (cf. John 1:18; 5:17-18; 19:7; see above). And second, in verse 27, they just heard Christ claim to be the unpredicated,[23] *egō eimi* ("I am"): "But immediately Jesus spoke to them, saying, "Take courage, *egō eimi* ['I am'], do not be afraid"). The same Greek phrase appears in Mark 6:50 and John 6:50 also records Jesus' *egō eimi* claim. Contextually unequivocal, they worshiped the Son of God, as God, the great "I am."

John 9:35-38: "[Jesus] said [to the blind man that He healed], 'Do you believe in the Son of Man?' He answered, 'Who is He, Lord, that I may believe in Him?' [37] **Jesus said to him, 'You have both seen Him, and He is the one who is talking with you.'** [38] **And he said, 'Lord, I believe.' And he worshiped [*proskuneō*] Him."** As in Matthew 14:33, the worship was combined with not one, but two divine titles. The blind man worshiped Christ as both the "Son of Man" and "Lord"[24] in a religious context, worshiped Christ as God.

Hebrews 1:6: "But when He [the Father] again brings his first-born into the world, He says, 'Let all the angels of God worship Him!'"[25] Undeniably, the context of the prologue of Hebrews presents the person of the Son, as God, worshiped by "all" the created angels, and the YHWH of Psalm 102:25-27, the Creator of all things. Yet the Bible of the JWs, The New World Translation (NWT) omits the term "worship" in Hebrews 1:6.[26] However, from the NWT's inception in 1950 (NT) to the 1970 edition, the NWT taught that Jesus (who JWs identify as Michael, the created archangel)[27] was worshiped by "all the angels." This caused a theological dilemma for the JWs. So, in the 1971 edition of the NWT, the Watchtower changed "worship" to "obeisance," which means "give honor, respect, homage, reverence," etc. removing the teaching that the Son of God was worshiped.

Although the Greek term ***proskuneō***[28] could mean either religious

---

23 "Unpredicated," meaning that the *egō eimi* ("I am") phrase contains no supplied predicate in the origi-nal, such as "*He*," or "the one I claimed to be," etc.

24 As seen, in note 24 above, Daniel 7:9-14 clearly indicates that the "Son of Man" is a divine title; this was also understood by the high priest in Mark 14:61-64. In the same breath, the blind man also addressed Christ as "Lord." As with the term *proskuneō* ("worship, obeisance, fall prostrate before another," etc.), the term *Kurios* ("Lord") is clearly expressed in a religious context—namely, Lord in the sense of true God.

25 This citation is from the LXX of Deuteronomy 32:43.

26 "But when He again brings his Firstborn into the inhabited earth, He says: "And let all of God's angels **do obeisance** to Him" (emphasis added).

27 As discussed below.

28 From *pros*, "toward," "with" + *kuneō*, "to kiss"; thus, "to prostrate oneself before persons and kissing

"worship" (reserved for God alone)[29] or "obeisance" (reverence) with no connotation of religious worship at all. However, as stated, context always determines the meaning of words and phrases. And as just said, the defining context of the prologue presents the Son as YHWH the unchangeable Creator, in contrast to all things created (viz., the earth, heavens, and all the angels). And to say again, the setting surrounding Hebrews 1:6 is in the heavenlies, hence, worship in a religious context. We will be examining the JWs in greater detail below.

Revelation 5:13-14: "And every created thing ... I heard saying, 'To Him who sits on the throne, and to the Lamb, be blessing and honor and glory and dominion forever and ever.' [14] **And the four living creatures kept saying, 'Amen' and the elders fell down and worshiped** [*proskuneō*]." Here the Father and the Lamb received the *same kind* of blessing, honor, and glory and thus, the same kind of worship, from **"every created thing."** Hence, the Lamb (Jesus) is excluded from the category of "created things." Rather, as in Hebrews 1:6, the Son was worshiped in a religious context, that is, as God. This revealing truth shows that the Son shares the very essence of God the Father. He is God in the same sense as that of the Father (cf. John 1:1, 18; Heb. 1:3).

IV. The Son is presented as the Creator of all things

John 1:3: "*Panta di' autou egeneto* ['all things through Him came into being'], and apart from Him nothing came into being that has come into being." The plain reading here as well as verse 10, indicates that the Word, Christ the Lord (John 1:4, 14, 18) was the Creator of all things. John specifically states that "all things" were created *di' autou*[30] ("through Him"). Grammatically, when the preposition *dia* ("through, by") is followed by the genitive case (as with *autou*, "Him"), it indicates agency.[31] The same prepositional phrase (*dia* + the genitive) is used at

---

their feet ... the ground," BDAG).

29 As in John 4:24.

30 In Greek, *dia* is written *di'* before a vowel (e.g., *di' autou*, "through Him"), except before proper names (e.g., *dia Iēsou* ("through Jesus," John 1:17) and except 2 Corinthians 5:7 and Romans 8:10.

31 In the NT, agency is commonly expressed in three ways: **ultimate agent** (the ultimate source of the action; the one directly responsible for the action—*apo, hupo, para,* + genitive); **intermediate agent** (that which the ultimate agent uses to carry out the action— *dia* + the genitive); and **impersonal agent** (that which the ultimate agent uses to perform the action—*en, ek* + the dative (GGBB, 431-32). Biblically, then, the Father was the source (ultimate agent) of creation, the Son being the intermediate agent in that He carried out the act for the ultimate agent (cf. ibid, 431). That the Son is the

John 1:10[32]; 1 Corinthians 8:6[33] and Hebrews 1:2,[34] which plainly and grammatically present the Son as the agent (intermediate) of creation, thus, the Creator of all things.[35]

Colossians 1:16-17: "That *en autō* ['by Him'] *ta panta* ['the all things'] were created both in the heavens and on earth, visible and invisible, whether thrones or dominions or rulers or authorities, *ta panta* ['the all things'] have been created *di' autou* ['through Him'] and *eis auton* ['for Him']. [17] He is *pro pantōn* ['before all things'], and *ta panta en autō* ['the all things in Him'] *sunestēken* ['hold together']."

1. Along with John 1:3, Paul employs the neuter adjective *panta* ["all things'], which indicates that the Son was the actual Creator of things (cf. Eph. 1:11). To reinforce his refutation, Paul definitizes[36] the adjective, *ta panta* ("the all things").

2. Paul utilizes four different prepositions to magnify his affirmation that Jesus the Son of God was the agent of creation: All things were created "by Him" (*en* + dative; vv. 16, 17); "through Him" (*dia* + genitive; v. 16); "for Him" (*eis* + accusative; v. 16); and, He is "before all things" (*pro* + genitive; v. 17).

3. As a final point, as shown in John 1:3, Paul specifically states that "the all things" were created *di' autou* ("through Him"). As observed above, the preposition *dia* is followed by the genitive grammatically revealing that the Son was the actual Creator Himself. There is no

---

intermediate agent of creation does not mean that He was a mere "helper" of sorts, or a secondary agent of God, but rather, He was the actual agent of creation—namely, that which the ultimate agent (the Father) used to carry out the action, thus, the Son is the Creator of all things. Ultimate or intermediate agent (or impersonal agent), is still an agent.

32 "He was in the world, and the world came into being **through Him** [*di' autou*] and yet the world did not know Him."

33 "Yet for us there is one God, the Father, from whom are all things and for whom we live, and one Lord, Jesus Christ, through whom are all things and **through whom** [*di' hou*] we live."

34 "In these last days [God the Father] has spoken to us in His Son, whom He appointed heir of all things, **through whom** [*di' hou*] also He made the world."

35 Regarding John 1:3, Robertson explains: By him (δι' αυτου). By means of him as the intermediate agent in the work of creation. The Logos is John's explanation of the creation of the universe. The author of Hebrews (Heb 1:2) names God's Son as the one "through whom he made the ages." Paul pointedly asserts that "the all things were created in him" (Christ) and "the all things stand created through him and unto him" (Col 1:16). Hence it is not a peculiar doctrine that John here enunciates. In 1 Co 8:6, Paul distinguishes between the Father as the primary source (εξ ου) of the all things and the Son as the intermediate agent as here (δι' ου) (*Word Pictures*, 1932: 5:5).

36 That is, Paul marks the adjective *panta* ("all things") with the article (ta, "the")— "the all things," which intensifies his polemic against the gnostics.

stronger way in which Paul could have articulated that the Son was the real and actual agent of creation.[37]

Hebrews 1:10-12. The Son is directly addressed by the Father as the Lord, that is, the YHWH of Psalm 102:25-27, the unchangeable Creator of all things. Hebrews 1:10-12 is discussed in detail below.

THE DIVINE SONSHIP IN THE PROLOGUE OF HEBREWS

The context of the prologue of Hebrews is a sharp contrast between all things created (heavens, earth, and angels) and the eternal divine Son. In verse 2, the Son is presented as the agent of creation, the Creator (as seen above). In verse 3, the Son "**is** [ōn, "always subsisting, being"] the radiance of His [the Father's] glory and the **exact representation** [*charaktēr*] of His **nature** [*hupostaseōs*]." No mere creature could make this claim. In verse 6, we read that the Father commands "**all** [*pantes*] the angels of God" to worship the Son. As seen above, in verse 6, we see that the Son is worshiped in a religious context—namely, worshiped as truly God. In verse 8, the Father directly addresses the Son as *ho Theos* ("the God") whose throne "is forever and ever." In verses 10-12, the Father attributes the creation of the heavens and the earth to the person of the Son (as in v. 2):

> And, "You, Lord, laid the foundation of the earth in the beginning, and the heavens are the work of your hands; [11] they will perish, but you remain; they will all wear out like a garment, [12] like a robe you will roll them up, like a garment they will be changed. But you are the same, and your years will have no end" (ESV).

God the Father is the speaker (cf. vv. 5-13). Verses 10-12 are cited

---

37 In regards to the Oneness view, which, as we will see below in our section on Oneness theology, the Word is seen as a plan or concept merely in view of the Father, but not as an eternal divine person. But if Paul wanted to convey the idea that the Son was merely a plan "in view" of the Father, or a conceptual instrument of creation (as in Oneness thinking), he certainly would not have used the linguistic prepositional phrase *dia* + the genitive, denoting actual agency, which militates against the Oneness notion of a non-preexisting conceptual idea of a Son mode.

from the LXX of Psalm 101:26-28 (Hebrew MT,[38] 102:25-27[39]) in which the Father attributes the creation of the heavens and the earth to the divine Son (as the author does in v. 2). These passages are devastating to groups that deny the deity of the Son as Creator of all things (esp. Muslims, unitarians, Oneness advocates and JWs).

In detail:

1. **"You, Lord."** In verses 5-13, the Father is speaking about or to the Son. In verse 8, the Father is directly addressing the Son: *Pros de ton Huion* ("But regarding [lit., 'towards'] the Son *He says*"). So, in verses 10-12, it is the same referential identity to whom the Father is addressing—the Son. There is no shift in the person from verses 5-9 and thus, verses 10-12—namely, the Father is addressing the Son: "You Lord." In fact, verse 10 starts with the Greek conjunction *kai* ("and"[40]), which naturally looks back to the addressee in verse 8: "But regarding the Son He says."

2. **Hebrews 1:10-12 is taken from the LXX of Psalm 102:25-27, which speaks of YHWH as the unchangeable Creator of all things.**

3. **The Father directly applies these passages in the Psalm to the Son, as the LORD (YHWH) of Psalm 102:25-27, the unchangeable Creator of all things.**

4. **The term "Lord" (as in "You Lord") appears in the actual vocative case (i.e., case of direct address)—*Kurie,* in the LXX of Psalm 102:25-27.** In verse 8, the noun *Theos* ("God"), although technically in the nominative (subject) case, it contextually carries the vocative force of *direct address.* In every occurrence in the NT where *Theos* (God) is being directly addressed, *Theos* appears in the nominative case, except in one passage, Matthew 27:46, where *Theos* appears twice in the vocative case (*Thee*): "My God [*Thee*], My God [*Thee*], why have You forsaken Me?" However, in Hebrews 1:10, "Lord" actually appears in the vocative form (*Kurie,* from *Kurios*) in the Greek: **"You [the Son], Lord [*Kurie*], in the beginning...."** The Father is not merely speaking "about" the Son; rather, He is directly addressing the Son— "You, Lord." Hebrews 1:10-12 utterly shatters the arguments of those who deny the Trinity and thus, deny the deity, unipersonality, and preexistence of the Son. Thus, God the Father is addressing the Son as both

---

38 Masoretic Text, which is the standard Hebrew text upon which most biblical translations are based.
39 The numeration of Psalms in the LXX is different from the Hebrew Masoretic Text.
40 *Kai Su kat' archas Kurie,* "And You in [the] beginning Lord."

ho Theos ("the God") whose throne is forever, and *Kurie,* that is, the YHWH ("Lord") of Psalm 102:25-27—the unchangeable Creator of all things.

The unique way in which Jesus claimed to be the Son of God in the Gospels was tantamount to His claiming to be *God the Son*—as clearly understood **by the Jews** (Mark 14:61-64; John 5:17-18; 19:7), **by the apostles** (Matt. 14:33; 16:18; John 1:1, 18; Rom. 1:3-4; **in the prologue of Hebrews**; 1 John 5:12, 20); **by the devil** (Matt. 4:3); **by demons** (Luke 4:41), and **by God the Father** (Matt. 3:17; 17:5; Heb. 1:6, 8-12).

In all these cases, we find Jesus' affirmation of being the "Son of God" was in a unique way— "the one and only [*monogenēs*] Son." His claims of deity were ascribed to neither men nor angels. Jesus' affirmation of being the Son of God was in turn a declaration that denoted ontological equality with God—the *monogenēs Theos* ("unique God," John 1:18). And the Jews clearly understood the implications of His claim: "For this reason therefore the Jews were seeking all the more to kill Him ... but also was calling God His own Father, making Himself equal with God.... For a good work we do not stone You, but for blasphemy; and because You, being a man, make Yourself out to be God... We have a law, and by that law He ought to die because He made Himself out to be the Son of God" (John 5:18; 10:33; 19:7). Both the OT and NT, present that the person of the Son, Jesus Christ was identified as YHWH, truly God and truly man, presented as the Creator of all things, and rightly worshiped as God—the Second Person of the Trinity!

COMMON OBJECTIONS TO THE DEITY OF CHRIST MADE BY UNITARIAN GROUPS

How can Jesus be God when the Bible says that there is only one God" (Deut. 6:4; Jer. 10:10-11).

Answer: As seen, "one God" does not mean "one person." Again, the Trinity teaches that God is one Being, and has revealed Himself in three distinct persons, *not three separate Gods.*

If Jesus were God, how could He have died? God can't die.

Answer: Jesus was God in the flesh. He has two natures; as truly God He is eternal being coequal and coexistent with the Father and Holy Spirit. As truly man, He was subject to sadness, hunger, pain, grief, etc. and death, "even death on a cross" (Phil. 2:8), but without sin.

In His mediatorial role, as truly man, He was the perfect representation of men, and as truly God, He was the perfect representation of God (1 Tim. 2:5). So, His physical body died on the cross (human nature), not His essential deity (divine nature).

If Jesus were God, why does He pray to God and refer to God as "My God"? (Matt. 27:46; John 20:17)?

Answer: Jeremiah 32:27: "Behold, I am the Lord, the God of all flesh...." Jesus as man, God (the Father) is His Lord and God, but as God, the Father addresses Him as "the God" (Heb. 1:8) and "Lord" (Heb. 1:10-12; viz., the YHWH of Ps. 102:25-27). Thus, Matthew 27:46 and John 20:17 are incarnational statements. As man, Jesus prayed to God the Father, and referred to Him as His God. In **Psalm 22:10**, which is speaking from the perspective of the coming Messiah, the palmist says: "I was cast upon You from birth; You have been my God from my mother's womb." So, from birth (His incarnation), the Father has been His God. Jesus is God in the flesh—two natures, God and man.

If Jesus were God, why does He say that the Father is "greater" than He is in John 14:28?

Answer: First, through John's literature Jesus is presented as truly God (John 1:1; 5:17-18; 8:58 17:5; 1 John 5:20 et al.). So, it would be contradictive for John to all of a sudden change his theology in John 14:28. In a few verses prior (v. 23), Jesus says that He and the Father will come to and make their home with all believers simultaneously. Hence, Jesus affirms His omnipresence—an attribute only God can accomplish. So, Jesus' statement that the Father is "greater" than Him, is not a denial of His deity.

It is an *economical* (functional) statement, not an *ontological* (in nature) one. In other words, the incarnate Son speaks of the Father's *greater* position, not His superiority in nature.

Contextually, as Wallace observes, "Jesus is speaking with reference to His office, not His person. That is, the Father has a greater rank, but the Son is no less deity than is the Father (cf. John 14:8). This is in line with one of the chief themes of the Fourth Gospel—to point out emphatically the deity of the Word."[41]

Lexically (i.e., meaning in its original significance), the term

---

41 GGBB, 111.

translated "greater" is from the Greek (comparative) adjective *meizōn*.[42] The lexical meaning of the term refers to "greater, larger, older, stricter, louder"—by virtue of position not "better" in nature. There is no standard lexicon that provides a meaning of ontological superiority at John 14:28.[43] In a similar sense is 1 Corinthians 11:3, which also speaks of position, not essence: "But I want you to realize that the head of every man is Christ, and the head of the woman is man, and the head of Christ is God." That man is the head of the woman, does not mean he is better or ontologically superior than her. The same could be said of the Father being *the head* of Christ, that is, greater than Him. The same *comparative* adjective (*meizōn*) is used in other places in the NT, denoting either age, position, or rank, and not ontological preeminence:

Luke 7:28: "I say to you, among those born of women there is no one **greater** [*meizōn*] than John; yet he who is least in the kingdom of God is **greater** [*meizōn*] than he" (emphasis added).

John 13:16: "Truly, truly, I say to you, a slave is not **greater** [*meizōn*] than his master, nor is one who is sent **greater** [*meizōn*] than the one who sent him" (cf. John 15:20; (emphasis added)—denoting a greater, more superior position, not greater in nature.

John 14:12: "Truly, truly, I say to you, he who believes in Me, the works that I do, he will do also; and **greater** [*meizōn*] works than these he will do; because I go to the Father"[44] (emphasis added).

James 3:1: "Let not many of you become teachers, my brethren, knowing that as such we will incur a **stricter** [*meizōn*] judgment" (emphasis added).

Romans 9:12-13 (from Gen. 25:23, LXX): "The LORD had said to Rebekah, 'The **older** [*meizōn*, Esau] will serve the younger [Jacob].' [13] Just as it is written, 'Jacob I loved, but Esau I hated'" (emphasis added).

If Jesus were God, why does He say that *only* God is good? "As He was setting out on a journey, a man ran up to Him and knelt before Him, and asked Him, 'Good Teacher, what shall I do to inherit eternal

---

42 The singular nominative masculine form of *megas*.
43 For example, BDAG sees the adjective as used in John 14:28, as "pert. to being relatively superior in importance, great."
44 Contextually, the greater works, merely meant greater in geography, not ontologically. When we examine the early chapters of Acts, from a purely numerical standpoint, the evangelism and deeds of Peter and the other apostles far surpassed (numerically greater) than those of Jesus in a single day (viz., the day of Pentecost). On that day, more were added to the church than had become followers of Christ during His entire earthly ministry of three years.

life?' 18 And Jesus said to him, 'Why do you call Me good? No one is good except God alone.'" (Mark 10:17-18).

Answer: First, the objection here assumes unitarianism (*God is one person*). Second, Jesus' statement that "only God is good," is not a denial of Him being God. It seems here that Jesus was trying to direct the man into questioning whether He really believed Jesus was absolutely good in the same sense that God is good. Yes, only God is good. And Jesus is infallibly and absolutely good. Consider these examples in the content of Mark, which presents this:

Mark 1:23-24: The demons had asked Christ: "What business do we have with each other, Jesus of Nazareth? Have You come to destroy us? I know who You are the Holy One of God!" To be the "Holy one of God," is absolutely good.

Mark 2:10: "'The Son of Man has authority on earth to forgive sins,' He said to the paralytic." That Jesus has the power to forgive sins is absolutely good!

Mark 10:45: "For even the Son of Man did not come to be served, but to serve, and to give His life a ransom for many." Again, this is absolutely good!

Mark 13:26-27: 26 And then they will see the Son of Man coming in clouds with great power and glory. 27 And then He will send forth the angels, and will gather together His elect from the four winds, from the end of the earth to the end of heaven." That the Son of Man sends *His angels* and gathers *His elect* is absolutely good, which only God can do. Scripture presents that only God has "elect" (Rom. 8:33; 11:5; Eph. 1:4-5; 2 Thess. 2:13). Further, in John 10:11, Jesus says, "I am the good shepherd; the good shepherd lays down His life for the sheep." This, is absolutely good. So true were the words of Christ, "only God is good." Christ is absolutely good, truly God.

If Jesus were God, why does He not know when He is coming back? "But about that day or hour no one knows, not even the angels in heaven, nor the Son, but the Father *alone*" (Mark 13:32).

Answer: First, there are many places in Scripture in the NT showing that Jesus indeed possesses omniscience (i.e., *all knowing*, John 2:24-25; 6:64; 16:30; 21:17 et al.). So how do we deal then with this passage and respond to the objectors?

There are two possible views within conservative scholarship:

1) Incarnational. God the Son *emptied Himself* (Phil. 2:6-8), which involved a veiling (not divesting) of *some* of His divine prerogatives.

This view would see Jesus in His incarnational state (as man) not *knowing* certain things, such as when He is coming back. This is a popular and plausible view, however, this view has a sticky point. The passage says that the Father *alone* knows. What about the Holy Spirit? Does He not know? He did not *empty* Himself. What would be the basis of His ignorance? For the passage clearly says, no one knows except "the Father *alone.*"

2) **"Know"** in the *preeminent sense.* This view, however, is unproblematic and consistent with the teaching of the Trinity. The simple response has to do with the verb *oiden* ("knows"). This verb (from *oida*) can be used in "preeminent sense," in that, the verb *oiden* takes the force of the Hebrew verbal stem *hiphil*—namely, seeing the action of the verb in a *causative or declarative sense*: "I make known, cause, promulgate, declare." The same base verb (*oida*) as in Mark 13:32 ("knows") is used this way in 1 Corinthians 2:2, where Paul states: **"I determined *to know* [*eidenai* from *oida*] nothing among you but Jesus Christ and him crucified,"** that is, *I cause, determined, or declare, to make known* **nothing among you, but Jesus Christ.** Therefore, in Mark 13:32, the verb can take this causative or declarative force—i.e., a "preeminent sense" (as in 1 Cor. 2:2). The **Son does know the day and hour of His return,** but the one who will make it known, cause, promulgate, declare it, is the Father alone.

A proper exegesis eliminates any notion of Christ being ignorant of His own return.[45] Although this view seems more probable, both views are consistent with entire content of the NT (and OT), which positively affirm Jesus Christ as truly God and truly man.

---

45 The sense would be: "Neither man nor angel, nor even the Son Himself, but the Father alone will make known, declare, cause you to know, the particular day and hour of the return of Christ (or destruction of Jerusalem); only He (in His preeminence) will reveal it to you."

FIVE

The Reliability of the New Testament

> [16] All Scripture is God breathed out and profitable for teaching, for reproof for correction, for training in righteousness [17] so that the man of God may be adequate, equipped for every good work (2 Tim. 3:16-17).

Throughout history, the veracity of the NT (as well as the OT) has been vociferously attacked by the secular world, non-Christian cults (e.g., LDS), and crass liberal scholarship (e.g., the Jesus Seminar). Yet, as consistently shown, the textual evidence for the NT is demonstratively greater than these works in terms of preservation and quantity. Baseless attacks on the reliability of the Bible (esp. the NT) are common. Thus, it is worth mentioning a few key points. Because of the vast number of Greek NT manuscripts, some significant ones dating back to the second century, it would be then impossible to sustain any argument of manuscript corruption as groups such as Islam and the LDS Church assert, as we will see below. To date, we have almost 6,000 extant Greek NT manuscripts. There are twenty-five or twenty-six possible second century Greek NT manuscripts (written on papyrus), which contain over 40% of the NT (e.g., P^4 [P^{64} + P^{67}] P^{20} P^{27} P^{32} P^{46} P^{52}, P^{66}, P^{75} P^{77} [P^{103}] P^{87}, P^{98}, P^{104}, P^{109}, P^{115}, P^{118}).[1] By the fourth century, the entire NT is represented in the manuscripts.

Currently, there are extant about 20,000-30,000 handwritten copies of the NT in other languages. The most significant of these ancient versions are the Syriac, Latin, Coptic (in the thousands), Gothic, Armenian, Georgian, and Ethiopic versions. Aside from that, there are other ancient versions in existence as well (such as Arabic). In fact, there are over 10,000 copies of the Latin Vulgate, and some NT Latin versions (viz. the Old Latin) date back (and prior) to A.D. 200. For example, Tertullian, Cyprian, and other ante-Nicene church Fathers wrote their works in Latin. So extensive were the writings of the early church Fathers that before the Council of Nicaea (A.D. 325), we have extant, roughly 36,000 quotations of the NT! *Incontrovertibly, the manuscript reliability and support for the NT documents far exceeds any other work of antiquity.* Notwithstanding the absence of the original autographs, the NT has been well preserved by the massive quantity of surviving Greek manuscripts. In effect, there are no significant differences (in terms of viable variants) in the readings of the earliest Greek NT manuscripts (from the second century) to the latest ones (fifteenth and sixteenth centuries) that affect any cardinal doctrine.[2]

So, we can say with confidence: All "recognized" biblical translations faithfully communicate the foundational truths of the gospel, that is, the person, nature, and finished work of Jesus Christ, God incarnate. John 1:1, for example, reads exactly the same (with no *viable*

---

1   Cf. Philip Comfort, *A Commentary on the Manuscripts and Text of the New Testament* (Grand Rapids, MI: Kregel Publications, 2015), 43ff.

2   Regarding the NT, there are four standard Greek NT editions upon which the various biblical translations are based: The **Textus Receptus** (the text of the KJV); the **Neutral Text** (or Westcott and Hort ed.); the **Majority/Byzantine Text** (or Ecclesiastical Text); and the **Critical Text** (or Eclectic Text, the Nestle-Aland 28th ed., and UBS 5th ed.). The CT however, is the current Greek NT edition from which most modern translations are based. Even between the Majority Text and CT, there exists only about 6,600 differences (Wallace). Hence, both editions are in 95% agreement, which is about 4.7% variation between these editions. To say again, none of the variants in the Greek NT editions affect any major Christian doctrine, because all chief doctrines of the Cristian faith are unaltered and intact.

variant reading[3]) in every single Greek NT manuscript, which contains it, from the earliest ones (P[66], P[75]), to the latest ones: *En archē ēn ho Logos, kai ho Logos ēn pros ton Theon, kai Theos ēn ho Logos* (lit., "In [the] beginning was the Word, and the Word was with the God, and God was the Word").

---

3   Dissimilar to every Greek NT manuscript containing John 1:1, there are two late eighth century manuscripts, Codex Regius (L) and Codex Washingtonianus (W) that contain the article before *Theos* in John 1:1c (*ho Theos, "the God* was the Word"). However, this late variant reading is seen as non-viable in that neither has textual (Greek or versional) merit nor patristic witness to constitute being even a probable variant. In other words, it lacks any likelihood of being an original reading The textual apparatuses of the CT (NA[28]) does not even list it as a possible variant reading.

Six

"Another Jesus"

A central and repeated theme within the writings of the Apostle Paul is the positive affirmation of the true deity and true humanity of Christ, and His substitutionary and sacrificial atoning work, which is Paul's "gospel." In fact, defending and affirming these important truths is a divine mandate to all Christians—especially pastors. Fully aware of the spiritual impact of false teachings regarding the person, nature, and finished work of Christ, Paul, while admonishing the Corinthian church, says:

But I am afraid that, as the serpent deceived Eve by his crafti-ness, your minds will be led astray from the simplicity and

> purity of devotion to Christ. For if one comes and preaches another Jesus whom we have not preached, or you receive a different spirit which you have not received, or a different gospel which you have not accepted, you bear this beautifully [*kalōs anechomai*, lit., 'well tolerate']...." (2 Cor. 11:3-4).

For such men that preach another Jesus and, thus, a different spirit and different gospel, are, as Paul says, "false apostles, deceitful workers, disguising themselves as apostles of Christ. No wonder, for even Satan disguises himself as an angel of light."

Therefore, it is not surprising if his servants also disguise themselves as servants of righteousness...." (vv. 13-15). As in modern times, Paul points out that many Christians bear (tolerate) well or are comfortable with those who preach "another" Christ—other than the Jesus of biblical revelation. Bearing with or tolerating a false Christology is sin, whether in ignorance or by deception. Further, Jesus stated, "true worshipers will worship the Father in spirit and truth. God is spirit, and those who worship Him must worship in spirit and truth" (John 4:23-24). Thus, worshiping a false Jesus and/or embracing a false or distorted gospel is not worshiping God in truth.

ATHEISTS

An atheist is one "without God" (from the privative *alpha* [*a*], "without, no," and *Theos,* "God"). Thus, an atheist is simply "without God," that is, without the true God. So theologically, all non-Christian religions are technically, "atheists"—being without God. For example, even though Ephesus was a center for the Artemis worship, Paul refers to Christians at Ephesus in their previous unconverted state, as *atheoi* ("atheists"): "That you *were at that time* without the Messiah, alienated from the citizenship of Israel and strangers to the covenants of promise, having no hope and *without God* [*atheoi*][1] in the world" (Eph. 2:12; emphasis added).

---

1 *Atheoi* is plural of *atheist.*

SIGNIFICANT CHRISTOLOGICAL HERESIES

The two major Christological heresies in the first century, which flow-ered in the following centuries, were the teachings of the **Judaizers** and **Gnosticism**[2] (proto-gnosticism[3]) especially the **docetic gnostics** (**Docetism**[4]). These seem to have had the greatest impact on the first century church. However, in the third and fourth century onward, **Modalism** (Oneness) and **Arianism** became some of the principal heresies to which the early Christian church responded by way of Councils, Creeds, and apologetic and polemic literature. Even today, however, these main Christological heresies although repackaged under different names, still live on and are well tolerated, and even endorsed, by unread "professing" Christians. Notice the theological parallels between the following groups: Judaizers then, now Roman Catholicism; Gnosticism then, now Christian/Religious Science (and many Word of Faith/charismatic churches have elements of this philosophy); Modalism then, now Oneness Pentecostalism (as well as some popular "professing" Christian authors and pastors such as **T. D. Jakes**, who embraces Oneness doctrine and thus, rejects the Trinity); Arianism then, now JWs and all other unitarian groups.

JUDAIZERS

As mentioned, the first known heresies of the first century church were the Judaizers and the Gnostics. The Judaizers were a group of seem-ingly professing Christians who taught that one needs to believe in the Messiah and (plus) conform to (practice) the Law of Moses (esp. circumcision). In the same way, as discussed below, *groups such as Roman Catholics, Eastern Orthodox, Church of Christ etc. confess Jesus as the Messiah, but reject justification through faith alone, apart from works*—as clearly taught in both the OT and NT (Gen. 15:6;

---

2   The term "Gnostic" (from the Greek term, *gnōsis*, "knowledge") was first used by the English poet and philosopher of religion Henry More (1614–87), who applied it to the religious groups referred to in ancient sources as the plural *gnostikoi*, which in Greek means, "those who have gnosis, or knowledge."

3   "Proto-gnosticism," since in the first century, the philosophy of Gnosticism was not yet a fully devel-oped system nor was any formal name attached to it.

4   "Docetism" referred to the philosophy of the early groups who denied Jesus' humanity, which was specifically refuted in 1 & 2 John. The docetic-gnostics viewed Jesus as non-physical, a phantom of sorts; only *seeming* to have a body. Serapion, bishop of Antioch, first used this description (*docetic,* c. A.D. 200), when he discovered the pseudepigraphic (false writing) *Gospel of Peter* during a pastoral visit to a Christian community using it in Rhosus, and later sharply condemned it as a forgery (thus, pseudepigraphic).

Acts 10:36, 43; Rom. 4:4-8; 5:1; Gal. 2:16 et al.).[5] The first ecumenical council at Jerusalem (Acts 15) addressed this erroneous doctrine, which caused much confusion among the early Christians there and was especially disturbing to the new converts. The opening statement at the Council at Jerusalem reads: "Some men came down from Judea and began teaching the brothers, 'Unless you are circumcised according to the custom of Moses, you cannot be saved'" (Acts 15:1). A denial of justification through faith alone was a fundamental gospel issue with Paul. He declared to the Christians in Galatia that it was "a gospel contrary to what we have preached" (Gal. 1:8-9). So heretical was the faith plus works theology of the Judaizers that Paul warns those who embrace it are *anathema* "accursed"[6] before God (ibid.).

Because of Peter's (along with Barnabas) hypocrisy, Paul rebuked him openly (Gal. 2:11-14). In fact, the only place in the NT where we find the term "Judaizer" is in Paul's rebuke (v. 14):

> [11] But when Cephas came to Antioch, I opposed him to his face, because he stood condemned. [12] For prior to the coming of some men from James, he used to eat with the Gentiles; but when they came, he began to withdraw and separate himself, fearing those from the circumcision. [13] The rest of the Jews joined him in hypocrisy, with the result that even Barnabas was carried away by their hypocrisy. [14] But when I saw that they were not straightforward about the truth of the gospel, I said to Cephas in the presence of all, "If you, being a Jew, live like the Gentiles and not like the Jews, how is it that you compel the Gentiles *to live like Jews*" (*Ioudaizō*, "to Judaize"; emphasis added).

---

5   Each of these groups teach the baptismal regeneration—namely, the idea that the "work" of water baptism is a necessary means of regeneration.

6   The Greek noun *anathema* is from *ana* ("up") and *tithēmi* ("to place, delver"). Thus, "a thing devoted delivered up to God for doom destruction without any hope of being redeemed" (Thayer; see also Lev. 27:28, 29; Josh. 6:17; 7:12 [LXX] et al).

GNOSTICISM (PROTO-GNOSTICISM, C. FIRST CENTURY)[7]

Whereas the Judaizing teaching was an attack on justification by faith alone, Gnosticism/Docetism was an attack on the real humanity of the person of Jesus Christ. The main idea with the Gnostic philosophy was that physical matter was illusory or inherently evil. The Gnostic Jesus was a non-physical *aeon* that emanated from the *plērōma* ("fullness") of the so-called "supreme God."

In this view, Jesus (as good aeon/god as they supposed) did not nor would not become or possess flesh, denying that He was God incarnate, the Creator of all things. The thought of Jesus as God incarnate was utterly repugnant to them. The main assertion of Gnosticism is the notion that Jesus was not God in the flesh, Creator of all things. Some gnostics asserted He only "appeared to have a body, but was actually spirit. Others asserted that Jesus was merely a human who attained a divinity (viz. the "Christ mind") at His baptism (as some taught) and through *gnōsis* ("knowledge") and taught His disciples to do the same. Their system of salvation consisted of obtaining this certain "knowledge," by which they could escape their "evil body." Hence, both Paul and the Apostle John specifically refuted all forms of this philosophy (e.g., Col. 1:14, 16-17; 2:8-9; 1 John 4:2-3; 2 John 1:7). Today, as mentioned, Christian Science (as with all Religious Science groups) hold to the same base philosophy. Scripture simply and clearly refutes this by the vast number of places that show that the person of Jesus Christ, the Son of God, was,

1. **God incarnate** (John 1:1, 14; Rom. 9:5; 1 Cor. 2:8; Phil. 2:6-11; Col. 2:9).
2. **Creator of all things**[8] (John 1:3; Col. 1:16-17; Heb. 1:2, 10-12).
3. **3. Perpetually (forever) God in the flesh** (John 1:18; Acts 1:11; 17:31; 1 Tim. 2:5; esp. 1 John 4:2-3; 2 John 1:7).

---

7   The greater part of information regarding Gnosticism is primarily drawn from the writings of Irenaeus, Hippolytus, Tertullian, Origen, and some later manuscripts discovered in the eighteenth century such as the Codex Askew, Codex Bruce, the Berlin Gnostic Codex, and the recent discoveries in the Nag Hammadi collection (1945). One of the most significant works addressing this system was by Irenaeus, Bishop of Lyons (c. 180), *The Refutation and Overthrow of the Knowledge Falsely So Called,* (cf. 1 Tim. 6:20).

8   That the Son as the actual Creator is discussed in detail below.

ARIUS OF ALEXANDRIA (FOURTH CENTURY)

In A.D. 318, in Alexandria, Egypt, confusion and tensions developed between professing Christians over a single, but rather essential point of theology, to the point of riots in the streets! It all started with a debate between Alexander, the bishop of Alexandria, and the determined presbyter Arius (A.D. 250-336). In A.D. 318, Arius was openly declaring that the Son was a "created" god of sorts, but not God (identical to the doctrine of the JWs). Hence, Arius assertively proclaimed: Ēn pote hote ouk ēn ("There was a time when He [the Son] was not"). Because of his unitarian belief (i.e., God existing as one person), Arius argued that if Jesus was God in the flesh that would indeed involve a change in the nature of God. For Arius, then, Jesus is "God," but only in a secondary sense, or, as God's representative on earth; not "God" in the same sense as that of the Father (again, similar to JWs). This was the chief issue at the Council of Nicaea (A.D. 325), which condemned him as a heretic and affirmed the orthodox view that the Son was *homoousios* ("same in substance") with God the Father. As stated in the resulting Creed, the Son was: "God of God, Light of Light, very God of very God begotten, not made, being of *one substance* [*homoousios*] with the Father by whom all things were made...." Today, as seen, the JWs (and other unitarian) are the modern day Arians holding to the same fundamental views (see below on our discussion of the JWs).

ISLAM (SEVENTH CENTURY)

As with all unitarian religious groups, Muslims reject the triune nature of God. Although, Muslims are taught that Jesus was the Messiah, a true prophet of Allah, sinless, virgin born, performed miracles, etc., they reject both the triune nature of God and that Jesus Christ was the eternal God in the flesh who was crucified and physically resurrected from the dead.

Response: The rejection of the deity of the Son, Jesus Christ (and the Trinity) is common to all "atheistic" non-Christian religions. As with JWs and Oneness Pentecostals, Muslims embrace a fixed unitarian/unipersonal assumption, that is, believing God to be one sole person. Mohammad, beyond question, was extraordinarily ignorant of Christian theology. For example, he thought the Trinity represented three separate gods, which is Tritheism, not Trinitarianism.[9] To assert that the Trinity is three separate Gods/gods is simply a typical straw-man fallacy that does not represent in any way, shape, or form the doctrine of the Trinity, biblically or historically. Mohammad's extreme biblical obliviousness especially on this issue is abounding throughout the pages of the Quran. The Quran speaks out against Tritheism (Sura 4:171; 5:73) and thus, not one word against proper Trinitarianism. Although **all unitarian groups assert God to be one person** (i.e., unipersonal), the Bible never speaks of God as one person, rather it presents God as one Being, revealed in three persons (not three Gods)—the Father, the Son, and the Holy Spirit, as discussed above.

It is corrupt, it is not corrupt. The Quran teaches that the "Gospel" (Injil or Injeel[10]) was "sent down" to Jesus by Allah[11] as "guidance and light" (5:46); the means of how the "people of the Book" (Christians) are to judge; and if anyone fails to use the Gospel to judge– "they are the ungodly" (5:47). In fact, the term Injil appears twelve times in the Quran (Sura 3:3, 48, 65; 5:46, 47, 66, 68, 110; 7:157; 9:111; 48:29; 57:27). So, it would seem simple to think that if any Muslim were to be diligent in their strict adherence to Allah in obeying his revelations, it would include accepting the Gospel. And thus, embracing its content—namely, the essential Christian doctrines, which are delineated in the four Gospels (esp. Jesus as Son of God, God in the flesh, Creator of all things, crucified and resurrected Savior, the only means of salvation, etc.). But this is not the case. When Christians attempt to evangelize the Muslim and proclaim the Jesus of the Gospels, the Muslim immediately goes to *default mode* arguing that the NT Gospels that Christians have in their hands today–is not the "Gospel" mentioned in the Quran; they do not identify it with the four canonical NT Gospels.

But what Gospel? Muslim scholars debate as to the exact nature of

---

9   Historically, these verses seem to be referring to a heretical so-called Christian sect called Mariyama or Collyridians who existed within the same geographical location and period as that of Mohammad. This sect held to a form of Tritheism, worshiping Mary and her Son, both of whom were believed to be two separate gods besides God.

10 Injil (or Injeel) is the Arabic translation of the Greek term, *evangelion* meaning, "good news, gospel."

11 Due to Mohammad's ignorance of the NT, he actually thought the Gospel was a book sent down to Jesus, rather than being a collection of four narrative books written by Jesus' followers (two of whom were close eyewitness companions) sometime after Jesus' ascension, who provided divinely inspired records of the teachings and actions of Christ. Many Muslims misinterpret Mark 1:1 to support Mohammad's claim.

the Injil (Gospel). The general view is that the original Gospel has been either corrupted beyond original recognition, lost, or elements of both. But very few Muslims are intelligently alive to the area of basic textual criticism to even sustain such an argument.

They typically argue in a circle, and/or point to "errors" and differences in translations, which, of course, have nothing to do with their claim that the actual NT (or OT) text was corrupted or altered. It is easy to see why the "lost" view is popular. Since the Quran teaches that the Gospel, which was allegedly "sent down" by Allah to Jesus, would not be nor could be corrupted (e.g., Sura 6:114-115), many modern Muslim scholars argue that Quranic Injil, that is, the Gospel, had simply been lost. Some Muslim scholars suppose that the NT Gospels and/or some other late non-biblical books (viz., pseudepigrapha, "false" books[12]), although corrupted, may contain some fragments of the original Injil,[13] which prompts the question: Upon what textual standard or criterion does a Muslim use to actually know which parts or "fragments" of the canonical Gospels are true, thus being part of the Quranic Injil? Classically, the Muslim may argue, if a passage in the NT teaches the deity of Christ or His cross work, then, it cannot be true, it must have been corrupted.

As pointed out above in chapter 5, regarding essential Christian doctrines, **there are no essential differences between the readings from that of the earliest NT manuscripts (second and third century) and latest ones (fifteenth and sixteenth century).** This means that the passages affirming the triune nature of God, the true deity and humanity of Jesus Christ including His unambiguous claims to be God, His atoning cross work (crucifixion, death, resurrection, ascension), and justification through faith alone *read principally the same in all Greek NT manuscripts at the places they appear—without any viable variant.* Of course, the corrupted and/or lost Injil theory was not an argument used by anyone, not even Mohammad.

For at that time, even until now, there is no evidence that such a claim has ever been made neither by Muslims, nor in the Quran, nor in any Christian source or literature. Seeing the glaring contradictions between the Quran and the NT Gospels (esp. in Sura 4:157), **Ibn Hazm,** a Muslim scholar and prolific author, first promulgated

---

12 Viz., "the Gospel of Childhood or the Nativity, the Gospel of Barnabas."
13 Cf. Abdullah Yusuf Ali, The Holy Qur-an: Text, Translation & Commentary (3rd ed.), 287.

the idea that the original Injil had been subsequently corrupted in the eleventh century![14] This means for the first four centuries of Islamic history, this doctrine of alleged corruption did not exist. The so-called corruption and the lost book theory are utterly vacuous of any historical evidence and was not posited by Muslims until four hundred years after Mohammad!

Peshitta. The Arab Christians and Jews who occupied land and cities in the Hijaz[15] (Mohammad's region) prior to Muhammad's existence, would have read and heard the Bible, not in the language of the region (Arabic). There was no Arabic translation of the Bible until the ninth century.[16] Rather, they would have used a Syriac translation of the Bible, the Peshitta.[17] So when Mohammad would make a reference to the "Gospel" in the Quran as being the "Book," "sent down" from Allah, being a "guidance and light," etc. it would have most certainly been from the Peshitta—the only biblical translation that the Christian possessed at the time of Mohammad. Again, for the first four centuries of Islamic history, this doctrine of an alleged corruption of the Injil did not exist. This is quite problematic for Muslims.

The Peshitta agrees (fundamentally) with all recognized standard OT and NT translations—especially on the true deity of Jesus Christ (e.g., Mark 14:61-64; John 1:1, 3, 14, 18; 5:17-18; 14:14; 8:58; 20:28; Rom. 9:5; Heb. 1:6, 8-12; 1 John 5:20 et al.; and the narrative accounts of the crucifixion, death, and physical resurrection of Jesus Christ). Therefore, Muslims have a great and unescapable dilemma: Allah promises in Sura 5:46 that the Gospel is (i.e., present tense) "guidance and light" and "guidance and instruction for the righteous." And Allah's words can never be changed nor altered (Sura 6:115). To stress the point again: The "lost" Gospel theory cannot be sustained being that historically the only book(s) that the Christians in that region and at that time had the canonical OT and NT. In other words, there is simply no evidence that the Christians (the so-called, "people of the Book") in the seventh century had a different Gospel than that of the four canonical NT Gospels.

---

14 Ibn Hazm, *Kitab Al-Fasl Fi Al-Milal Wa-Al-Ahwa' Wa-Al-Nihal* (Arabic ed.), vol. II, 6, 55, 64.

15 Western Saudi Arabia.

16 The earliest Arabic translation of the Bible known is the Codex Sinai (viz., Sinai Arabic Codex 151, A.D. 867).

17 Peshitta (and its variant spelling) means *simple* or *common* version. Most scholars date the earliest editions of the Peshitta around the third century, which contained twenty-two NT books minus 2 Peter; 2 and 3 John, Jude, and Revelation.

ROMAN CATHOLICISM (THE
MODERN DAY JUDAIZERS)

The Jesus of Romanism is an impotent Savior whose atoning cross work was anything but sufficient. Rome teaches that the work of Christ merely made a "way" for man to justify himself by adding to the work of Christ by performing "required" meritorious creaturely works (such as water baptism, charity, religious devotion [viz. *hyperdulia*] to Mary, submitting to Rome, etc.). Hence, Rome has man assisting Christ in salvation—hence denying that Christ alone saves. **Rome's auto-soteric (self-salvation) system is a system of "and's," for example:**

- God's universal plan *and* man's so-called free will.
- Faith *and* (or plus) works such as water baptism, sacraments, holding to all the Marian doctrines, *fides implicita* (viz., an uncritical faith in the Roman Catholic Church).
- Jesus *and* Mary.
- Intersession and prayers to Jesus and Mary (and so called saints).
- The cross *and* the perpetual sacrifices of Christ at the Mass.
- Biblical doctrine *and* the Church.
- Scripture *and* so-called Tradition of uninspired men.
- Christ *and* the Pope, etc.

Contrary to the biblical doctrine of Christ alone, the Christ of Rome is anything, but a powerful Savior. That Christ could not nor does not save alone, is a shared cross work that Rome embraces. Hence, Rome asserts a false Christ who did not become perfect man nor did He become the righteousness of all who believe (John 1:14; Phil. 2:7-8; 1 Cor. 1:30-31).

Response: In biblical opposition to Rome's doctrines, which so greatly oppose so many fundamental biblical teachings, especially on justification and the atonement.[18] For example:

---

18 Rome's denial of justification though faith alone, apart from works, leaves the Roman Catholic has no absolute assurance of (salvation) justification before the Lord, in this life nor glorification in the afterlife. According to Rome, a so-called "saved" person now could always forfeit his or her justified status by a lack of performance (esp. unconfessed mortal sins). Countering Rome's claim, the Bible is abounding with passages that teach that justification is a one-time permanent *objective* declaratory act of God pronouncing (not making) a sinner, through the instrument of faith, not guilty, just/righteous (Rom. 4:6-8; 5:1). A regenerated justified Christian is sealed for the day of eternity, in which as Christ

Mary. The Roman Church is a life embracing and practicing perpetual idolatry in giving Mary what is reserved for God alone—namely, religious worship. Generally, because of Roman Catholic tradition, Roman apologists lack greatly as to the lexical-semantic of the Greek noun *douleia* (Latin, *dulia*) and the verb douleuō in a religious context—in both in the OT (LXX) and NT. Simple rejoinder here, which does not require a lengthy corrective. To avoid the charge of idolatrous worship to Mary, Rome has developed a three-tier scheme in which they distinguish between so-called service or honor given to Saints and Mary, and worship given to God denoted by three Latin terms: *dulia* (service, given to so-called saints), *hyper-dulia* (super-service, given to Mary), and *latreia* (worship, given to God).

- **Dulia,** from the Greek noun, *duleia* (slavery, bondage, service), the verb being *douleuō* meaning, "to serve, be enslaved, in bondage"), which is given to all so-called saints (veneration).
- **Hyper-dulia** ("super/superior slavery, service") given to Mary alone.
- **Latria** from the Greek noun, *latreia* ("the service or worship of God" (Rom. 12:1; Heb. 9:1), and the verb being *latreuō*, "to give religious honor, worship" (cf. Dan. 7:14; Luke 4:8; Phil. 3:3; Heb. 9:14), which is reserved for God alone.

This distinction of three kinds of service/worship biblically is not valid.

First, Scripture nowhere teaches that faithful Christians should give *dulia* (Greek, *duleia*) and especially the Roman concocted term, *hyper-dulia* to creatures, in a religious context. Second, this distinction of three kinds of service/worship is biblically invalid. Semantically, to give *dulia* to anyone in a religious context is the same as giving *latria* (Greek, *latreia*)—they both denote worship reserved for God alone. Hence, by Catholics praying to creatures giving them *dulia* (religious veneration), bowing before statues of Mary is the very thing in which

---

promised, all the ones the Father gave to Him (John 6:37), "I lose nothing but, raise it up at the last day" (John 6:39, cf. v. 44). In Romans 4:8, Paul states that there is not even a possibility that the one justified by faith apart from works, God would credit (or impute, from *logizomai*) any sin against him (in the context of justification). Even more passages such as John 5:24; 10:28; 11:26; Romans 8:1, 28-39; 1 Corinthians 1:30-31; 2 Thessalonians 2:13; 1 John 5:12; Hebrews 13:5 exegetically affirm the perseverance and preservation of true believers *against* Rome's unbiblical soteriology.

God prohibits.[19] Paul strongly expresses this point in Galatians 4:8, **"When you did not know God, you were slaves ['you served,' from** *douleuō*] **to those which by nature are no gods."** Paul was clear: "to serve" (i.e., to give *douleia, dulia*) anyone other than God in a religious context is biblically wrong—it is patent idolatry. Paul sees the unconverted pagans as doing this: "When you did not know God"—you were giving *dulia* to creatures.[20]

The Idolatry of Rome's Marian Doctrines. Alphonsus Liguori, was a "Canonized Saint" (1839), and declared a "Doctor of the Church" in 1871 by Pope Pius IX. Historically, the Roman Catholic Church has named 37 Doctors of the Church (beginning with Irenaeus, A.D. 180).

The so-called Saint and Doctor of Roman Theology, Alphonsus Liguori, writes in his renowned massive book, *The Glories of Mary:*

"On account of the merits of Jesus, the great privilege has been granted to Mary to be the mediatrix of our salvation" (169).

"So, says St. Bernard, We have access to Jesus Christ only through Mary. And St. Bernard gives us the reason why the Lord decreed that all men should be saved by the intercession of Mary, namely that through Mary we might be received by that Saviour who, through Mary, has been given to us" (191-92).

"If you ever wish for another advocate with this mediator, invoke Mary, for she will intercede for you with the Son.... St. Bonaventure, too: He who neglects the service of Mary shall die in sin ... He who has not recourse to thee, oh Lady, will not reach paradise.... That those from whom Mary turns away her face, not only will [they] not be saved, but can have no hope of salvation" (228, 256).

---

19 Regarding idols and false gods, God commands His people in Exodus 20:5: "You shall not worship them or serve them; for I the LORD your God, am a jealous God." The Hebrew word translated "serve" (NASB, ESV, KJV, etc.) is from *abad* ("to work, serve"), which is the most common English translation of the term. In a religious context, *to serve* God is the same as *worshiping* Him—an action reserved for God alone (cf. Exod. 4:23; 7:16; *20:5;* Job 21:15; Mal. 3:18). In many OT passages, however, there are more than a few standard translations that translate *abad* as "worship" (e.g., NASB at Exod. 20:5; Ps. 2:11; Isa. 19:23; Jer. 35:15 et al.). The NIV translates *abad* as "worship" at Exodus 20:5: "You shall not bow down to them or **worship** them" (same at Exod. 3:12; Isa. 19:23 et al.). In the LXX, *abad* is frequently translated as *latreuō* ("to worship, serve"; Exod. 3:12; 20:5; etc.) and sometimes as *douleuō* ("to serve"; Isa. 19:23). In other words, in a religious context, both *latreuō* and *douleuō* (*to worship* or *to serve*) means the same thing—divine worship.

20 Cf. as discussed in note 89 above.

"Mary is called the Gate of Heaven, because no one can enter into heaven, as St. Bonaventure declares, except through Mary" (744).

These are only a few samples of authoritative Roman Catholic voices affirming Rome's distinctive Marian doctrines. These doctrines are purely outside of the Scripture; the NT knows nothing of this. In fact, aside from a passing reference in Galatians 4:4 of Jesus being born of a virgin (without mentioning Mary by name), after Acts 1:14, Mary is never mentioned again in any NT Epistle. Neither Jesus, nor any of His disciples, nor any NT Apostle prayed to her or referred to Mary as "Our Queen, "Our Life," "Our Hope," Our Mediatress, Our Advocate, Our Salvation, etc.

Transubstantiation. Roman Catholicism teaches that when Jesus said "'Do this in remembrance of me,' he gave the apostles and hence his future priests the power to change bread and wine into his body and blood" (*Baltimore Catechism,* Q. 354). The *Catechism of the Catholic Church* (CCC, para. 1413) also states: "Under the consecrated species of bread and wine Christ himself, living and glorious, is present in a true, real, and substantial manner: his **Body and his Blood,** *with his soul and his divinity"* (emphasis added). This change of the elements of the Eucharist (bread and wine) is an ontological (in actual nature) change.

Two fundamental heresies of Transubstantiation

1. Rejection of the once for all time atoning sacrifice of Christ as the very ground of justification. The Eucharist (also called, "Holy Communion") "re-presents" over and over the sacrifice (i.e., His cross work) of Christ. This denies the one-time finished atoning sacrificial cross work of Christ as the ground of justification. Rome repetitiously uses, for example, terms such as "sacrifice," "re-presents," "propitiatory" defining the effects of the Eucharist. Even though the NT never indicates that the Lord's Supper is a *perpetual* sacrifice, Rome says, "the Eucharist is thus a sacrifice because it re-presents (makes present) the sacrifice of the cross" (CCC, para 1366).

Rome teaches that the Eucharist is the *same as* the sacrifice of Christ, that is, propitiatory: **"The sacrifice of Christ and the sacrifice of the Eucharist are one single sacrifice.... This sacrifice is truly**

propitiatory" (CCC, para 1367).[21] Yet to say again, the NT never refers the Lord's Supper as propitiatory or a re-presented sacrifice. This Roman idea militates against the biblical teaching of the efficacy and sufficiency of the *once for all time* atoning work of Christ.

2. Transubstantiation deforms and thus, denies the Incarnation of the Son. Transubstantiation involves an "ontological" change to the bread and wine becoming (i.e., ontologically transforming into) Jesus' literal body and his blood ("with his soul and his divinity," as cited above). This Roman doctrine deforms and thus, rejects the perfect incarnation of the Son. Day after day millions of Catholics around the world receive the Eucharist at the Mass, in which *simultaneously* they eat, according to Rome, the literal body and drink the literal blood of Christ. This clearly implies that Jesus' physical body is ubiquitous—namely, it's in multiple places at the same time! A ubiquitous anomalous human nature of the Son sharply counters the biblical teaching that the eternal Word became the perfect representation of man—not a "hyper-flesh," that is, a ubiquitous fleshly body: "The Word became flesh" (John 1:14); "having been made [*genomenos*] in the likeness of men.

Having been found [*heuretheis*] in appearance as a man" (Phil. 2:7-8; cf. also Rom. 9:5; 2 Tim. 2:8). Along with the vast heretical Roman Catholic doctrines such as baptismal regeneration, purgatory, the idolatrous Marian doctrines, Rome's teaching of a transubstantial Eucharist mutilates the biblical view of the incarnation of the Son. It also rejects that salvation is through faith alone by Christ alone. Whereas biblical Christianity teaches that Scripture alone is our final authority, and salvation is by grace alone, through faith alone, by Christ alone, and for the glory of God alone—*Soli Deo Gloria!* Paul declares clearly that it is "by His doing you are in Christ Jesus, who became to us wisdom from God, and righteousness and sanctification, and redemption" (1 Cor. 1:30). Therefore, a Christ who did not become our righteousness, as Rome teaches, is not the Christ that Paul preached, whose

---

21 Even more, Question 343 of the **Baltimore Catechism** asks: "What is the Holy Eucharist? The Holy Eucharist is a sacrament and a sacrifice." Also see Questions 357, 358, and 360 teaching the same. The NT never refers to the Lord's Supper as a "sacrifice" or "propitiatory." Contra Rome's view, Paul defines the Lord's Supper is a remembrance ceremony of the one-time sacrifice of Christ—being the very ground or cause of justification (1 Cor. 11:23-44). *The Westminster Confession of Faith* expresses that "The elements (bread and wine) "are holy signs and seals of the covenant of grace, immediately instituted by God, to represent Christ and His benefits" (27:1). Hence, the elements signify the benefits of His one-time unrepeated sacrifice (1 Cor. 10:16).

cross work is the ground of justification (John 1:13; 6:37; 10:28; Acts 10:36, 43; 13:48; Rom. 4:4-8; 8:29-30; 9:16; Eph. 2:8-10; 2 Thess. 2:13; Titus 3:3-7)—not by any works:

- **Romans 4:6:** "God credits [or imputes] righteousness apart from works."
- **Romans 5:1-2:** "Therefore, since we have been declared righteous by faith, we have peace with God through our Lord Jesus Christ, [2] through whom we have also obtained access by faith into this grace in which we stand, and we rejoice in the hope of God's glory" (NET).
- **Ephesians 2:8-9:** "For by grace you have been saved through faith; and this is not of yourselves, it is the gift of God; [9] not a result of works, so that no one may boast."
- **2 Timothy 1:9:** "who saved us and called us with a holy calling, not according to our works, but according to His own purpose and grace, which was granted to us in Christ Jesus from all eternity."

To emphasize the completed redemptive propitiatory work of Christ, the author of Hebrews uses the Greek adverb *ephapax,* which means "once for all" (from *epi,* + *hapax,* "once, one"). The term means (lexically), "Taking place once and to the exclusion of any further occurrence, once for all, once and never again (BDAG), or "upon one occasion only" (Thayer). The author of Hebrews (and Paul in Rom. 6:10) teaches that the sacrifice of Christ as the eternal priest was *ephapax* ("once for all time")—for all other OT priestly systems (Aaronic, Levitical) were lesser, imperfect, and obsolete (Heb. 7:11, 23-28). Note the following passages:

- **Hebrews 7:27:** "who does not need daily, like those high priests, to offer up sacrifices, first for His own sins and then for the sins of the people, because this He did *ephapax* ['once for all time'] when He offered up Himself."
- **Hebrews 9:12:** "And not through the blood of goats and calves, but through His own blood, He entered the holy place *ephapax* ['once for all time'] having obtained eternal redemption."
- **Hebrews 10:10-14:** [10] "By this will we have been sanctified through the offering of the body of Jesus Christ *ephapax*

['once for all time'!].[11] Every priest stands daily ministering and offering time after time the same sacrifices, which can never take away sins; [12] but He, having offered one sacrifice for sins for all time, SAT DOWN AT THE RIGHT HAND OF GOD, [13] waiting from that time onward UNTIL HIS ENEMIES BE MADE A FOOTSTOOL FOR HIS FEET. [14] For by one offering He has perfected for all time those who are sanctified" (Heb. 10:10-14). Clearly shown, Roman Catholicism denies and rejects the Christian faith. Along with the list of other heresies not mentioned here, she rejects the once for all time finished atoning work of the Son, distorts the biblical doctrine of incarnation, and engages in extreme idolatry by giving Mary "hyperdulia," that is, religious super-service (viz. worship) reserved for God alone (Exod. 20:5; Gal. 4:8).

Also consider this, by praying to Mary and so-called Saints with the assumption that they actually hear, Rome accredits the exclusively divine attribute of omniscience to creatures!

The "Rock" of Matthew 16:18 – The Foundation of Rome

"I also say to you that you are Peter, and upon this rock I will build My church; and the gates of Hades will not overpower it."

This passage is Rome's basis of the Roman dogma of Papal Succession. Just as the foundation of the false church of the Latter-Day Saints raises and falls on Joseph Smith's First Vision, **the Romish Catholic Church, rises and falls on the Papal Succession**, which is the so-called divine transmission of ultimate spiritual authority from the Apostle Peter through successive Romish Popes. As with the atrocious false doctrine of ontological Transubstantiation, Rome sees Papal Succession in a real and literal way. The Romish doctrine that the Roman Pope carries the authority and infallibility of the biblical Apostles is called by Rome: *Ex Cathedra* ("from the chair"), which was officially made Dogma not until 1870 at Vatican 1, under Pope Pius

IX.[22] If Rome's infallible Papal Succession doctrine is biblical, then not only would it be supported by exegesis of the text at Matthew 16:18, but it would be historically shown that no Pope speaking officially, that is, "from the Chair" has ever erred.

However, on both counts, Rome's doctrine of Papal Succession fails. For example, there have been heretical Popes such as Honorius I (625- 638), who after his death, was Anathematized, for embracing Monothelitism (Christ as having "one will") and then later was Anathematized for not ending it. He was even officially named a heretic and Anathematized by the Third Council of Constantinople (680), and Pope Leo II (682- to death 683) endorsed the condemnation of him, as did later Popes. Pope Leo declared that Honorius, "allowed the immaculate faith to be stained" by teaching not "in accord with apostolic tradition."[23]

Before examining this text in detail, we must consider three important points in Jesus' response to Peter.

1. The context is not Peter, rather, the identification of Christ ("Who do you say that I am?" v. 13).

2. Peter's confession ("You are the Christ the Son of the living God") was of a divine origin, thus, not of himself (cf. Phil. 1:29). In Matthew 16:17, we read: "And Jesus said to him, "Blessed are you, Simon Barjona, because flesh and blood did not reveal this to you, but My Father who is in heaven."

3. Exegetically and the *general consensus* of the early church, according to Jesus, it was Peter's confession that was the "rock," upon which Jesus will build His church. Conversely, Rome asserts that the "rock" upon which Jesus will build His church is the Apostle Peter, and not his confession. The Roman interpretation of Matthew 16:18 is false both exegetically and historically, and problematic and unsupported.

Exegetically. The passage reads: *kagō de soi legō* ['I also now to you say'] that *su ei Petros* ["that You are Peter"] and *epi tautē tē petra*

---

22 *Ex Cathedra:* Any doctrines of "faith or morals" promulgated by the Pope–in his capacity as Successor to St. Peter, speaking from the Chair or Seat of his Episcopal authority in Rome is infallible, he cannot err. The Holy Spirit protects him from erring. The Nature of Infallibility was Stated in Session 4, Constitution on the Church 4, Vat 1.

23 Philip Schaff, "The Heresy of Honorius" in the *History of the Christian Church,* Vol. 4 (Grand Rapids, MI: Christian Classics Ethereal Library; First Published: 1882).

('upon this the rock') I will build My church, and the gates of Hades will not overpower it." As shown in the context which surrounds Jesus' statement to Peter (v. 18), starts in verses 13-15 with Jesus' question to His disciples regarding His identity: "But who do you say that I am?" It is Peter's response (v. 16), that is, His confession of who Jesus is ("the Christ, the Son of the living God") that stimulates Jesus' statement to Peter. Again, in verse 17, Jesus confirms that Peter's confession was *not derived* from Peter himself (not "flesh and blood")—rather it was revealed by God the Father.

"You" vs the phrase "this the rock." "I also now to "YOU" [*soi*] say that "YOU" [*su*] are Peter" (lit.). The two pronouns "YOU" (*soi* and *su*) are singular **second-person** personal pronouns. Thus, the pronouns are in direct reference—hence, Jesus is directly addressing Peter. Jesus *said to him*, not *about him*. Especially revealed in the next phrase (lit.): "And upon THIS [*epi tautē*] the rock, I will build my church." The demonstrative pronoun "THIS" (*tautē*) has a third person significance, that is, *indirect* address,[24] in distinction to the two second-person pronouns ("I also say **to you** [*soi*] that **you** [*su*] are Peter"). So, Jesus is not directly addressing the rock, but rather He is directly addressing Peter: "I say to "YOU, that YOU are Peter and upon THIS [not you] the rock I will build My church."[25] *Question:* If Jesus had wanted to directly identify Peter as the rock, why use the demonstrative pronoun "THIS" at all? For Jesus had already used two second-person pronouns (*soi, su,* "you") to directly address Peter. If Jesus had meant what modern-day Catholics assert, He simply would have stated to Peter: *epi sou tē petra* ("upon YOU the rock, I will build My church" or "You Peter are the rock," but He did not. Rather, "Upon THIS the rock I will build My church."

Historically. Many Catholics selectively quote (snippet) Patristics as agreeing with Rome's view (esp., Origen, Cyprian, and Eusebius, and Augustine, but citing only his early teachings; yet none of these church Fathers held to Rome's view). In fact, most Roman Catholics are not aware of the historical research done by Roman Catholic **Archbishop Peter Richard Kenrick** regarding the early church's view of Matthew

---

24 Although demonstrative pronouns ("this, that") do not grammatically have "person," they can express an *indirect* significance similar to a third person pronoun. They can express a thing ("this") other than a direct reference.

25 In Greek, *petros* means, "piece of rock"; while *petra,* means, "large stone, rock, mass." However, I do not see this distinction as a strong argument against Rome's view.

16:18. Kenrick prepared a paper on this subject, which was to be delivered to Vatican I (1870). However, it was never delivered, but it was published later, along with other insights.[26] He points out the five interpretations of the identification of the rock in Matthew 16:18, to which important Fathers of antiquity held.

1. **All Christians were the living stones.** This view was held by very few church Fathers. Origen, who is a common source of Patristic Tradition, states: "If we also say "You are the Christ, the Son of the living God," then we also become Peter ... for whoever assimilates to Christ, becomes rock. Does Christ give the keys of the kingdom to Peter alone, whereas other blessed people cannot receive them?" (Origen, *Commentary on Matthew*).
2. **All the apostles**—eight Fathers (Cyprian et al.).
3. **Christ as the rock**—sixteen Fathers (Eusebius, early Augustine). Eusebius of Caesarea (A.D. 263-339), in his view (i.e., the rock as Christ), links this interpretation with the parallel rock and foundation statements of 1 Corinthians 3:11 and 10:4.
4. **Peter as the rock**—only seventeen Fathers!
5. **The rock upon which the Church was built was the faith that Peter confessed—forty-four Fathers!** including the most significant Fathers (e.g., Basil of Seleucia, Cyril of Alexandria, Chrysostom, Ambrose, Hilary,[27] Jerome, Augustine who stated (later in life) in his *Retractions*:

> Christ, you see, built his Church not on a man but on Peter's confession. What is Peter's confession? "You are the Christ, the Son of the living God." There's the rock for you,– there's the foundation, there's where the Church has been built, which the gates of the underworld cannot conquer.

Thus, only twenty percent of the Fathers held to Rome's now

---

26 Cf. *An Inside View at Vatican I*, ed. Leonard Woolsey Bacon (New York: American Tract Society, 1871).
27 Hilary of Poitiers, *On the Trinity* (Book II): "Thus our one immovable foundation, our one blissful rock of faith, is the confession from Peter's mouth, Thou art the Son of the living God" (*On the Trinity*).

canonized "infallible" "Petrine Rock" interpretation of Matthew 16:18. That is far from being the norm of the early church. So, Kendrick himself concluded:

> If we are bound to follow the majority of the fathers in this thing, then we are bound to hold for certain that the 'rock' should be understood the faith professed by Peter, not Peter professing the faith.

As Roman Catholic apologist, H. Burn-Murdock actually admitted: "None of the writings of the first two centuries describe St. Peter as a bishop of Rome."[28] In fact, no one before Bishop Callistus (A.D. 223) ever used Matthew 16:18 to support the primacy of the Roman Bishop (i.e., "Pope" as Rome calls it)—*no one*. Lastly, consider the following points that seriously challenge Rome's position of the so-called Primacy of Peter and him being the first Pope of Rome:

1. There is no biblical evidence indicating that Peter had supremacy over all the other apostles.
2. Peter never once considered that he was Pope, Pontiff, Vicar of Christ, Holy Father, or Head of the whole Christian Church, nor did any of the other apostles make such as claim.
3. Peter outwardly denied the Lord (out of fear) and Peter was rebuked by the Apostle Paul for being prejudice against the Gentiles (cf. Gal. 2:11-12).
4. At the first church council in Jerusalem (not Rome), it was James and not Peter who was the leading speaker and decision maker, for James authoritatively declared Acts 15:19: "It is my judgment that we do not trouble those who are turning to God from among the Gentiles." Moreover, the letter that was sent out regarding the judgment never mentions Peter (cf. v. 23).
5. At the end of Romans (A.D. 57), Paul sends his greetings to at least twenty-eight people, but Peter is not even mentioned! Why? Surely, if Peter had "recognized supremacy" over Rome and all the apostles, we would expect Paul to have greeted him first!

---

28 H. Burn-Murdock, *The Development of the Papacy* (1954), 130f.

6. Peter was a married man, unlike the Roman Popes (cf. Matt. 8:14; 1 Cor. 9:5).

ONENESS THEOLOGY[29]

Oneness churches are characterized by and go by many names such as *Jesus Only*, Apostolic churches, Oneness Pentecostal,[30] Bethel, etc. Today, the largest Oneness denomination is the United Pentecostal Church International (UPCI). All Oneness advocates reject the Trinity. Rather they believe God is unitarian or unipersonal (one person). The name of the one God is "Jesus," who is both the Father/ Holy Spirit and Son. Oneness advocates claim that Jesus has two natures (or modes, manifestations, roles, etc.), divine as the Father/ Holy Spirit and human as the "non-divine," "non-eternal" Son, whose life started in Bethlehem. In this sense, the "Son" was created in the womb of Mary and is not eternal. In the Oneness doctrinal system then, the terms "Father," "Son," and "Holy Spirit" are not three persons, but rather the three roles or modes in which Jesus manifested.

Although not all Oneness advocates agree on every point of Christology, all forms are a clear and major departure from biblical orthodoxy. Oneness doctrine rejects the personhood, deity, and incarnation of the Son. Many Oneness denominations also reject that justification is through faith alone, not by works, by teaching that the *work* of water baptism is necessary for salvation (e.g., UPCI).

The chief Oneness Christological divergences from that of the biblical teachings are as follows:

- **Oneness Christology denies the unipersonality of the Son, Jesus Christ.**

---

29 Historically, Oneness philosophy first emerged around the early second and early third century being popularized by Noetus of Smyrna and Praxeas (Asia minor). It was also called Modalism since all forms of the Oneness idea saw God has merely appearing in three modes (or roles) as Father, Son, and Holy Spirit, but not in three persons. Subsequently, **Sabellianism became a popular brand Modalism**. Sabellianism was coined after its chief proponent, Sabellius, the Libyan priest who came to Rome at the beginning of the third century A.D. However, he taught *successive* Modalism, which saw the modes as successive, that is, "Jesus" (the name of the unipersonal God) first was the Father in creation, then, the Son in redemption, then the Holy Spirit in regeneration. In distinction to *simultaneous* Modalism, which teaches that all three modes exist at the same time. But the fact is, fundamentally, all forms historically and today are as unitarian (seeing God as one person), as with Islam's view of Allah and JWs' view of Jehovah.

30 Generally, there are two kinds of "Pentecostal" churches – Oneness (such as the UPCI) and *Christian* Pentecostal, which are Trinitarian (such as the AOG, Foursquare et al.).

- **Oneness Christology denies that the person of the "Son" is God.** As stated, Oneness theology teaches that Jesus' divine nature represents the Father and Holy Spirit, but not the Son, that is, the "Son" is not God; the Son is merely the human nature/mode of the unitarian deity, Jesus.[31]
- **Oneness Christology denies the preexistence and incarnation of the person of the Son and His role as the agent of creation, hence, the Creator of all things.**[32] **By** denying the preexistence of the person of the Son of God, Oneness doctrine rejects the incarnation of the divine Son holding to the erroneous notion that it was Jesus as the Father, not the Son, who came down and wrapped Himself in flesh (while not actually becoming flesh), and that flesh body was called "Son."[33]
- **Oneness Christology claims that Jesus is the Father, Son, and Holy Spirit (same person), hence denying the concept of the Trinity.**[34] Oneness theology is "unitarian" seeing God as a unipersonal deity.

Since Oneness theology maintains that only Jesus *as the Father* is God (for "Son" only represents the humanity of Jesus), it clearly denies the Trinity and deity and preexistence of the Son. As said, God is defined from a unitarian perspective: Only the Father is God (i.e., Jesus' divine nature). Clearly, Oneness theology is heterodox embracing a false Jesus, different from the Jesus of biblical revelation: **"Whoever denies the Son does not have the Father"** (1 John 2:23). Oneness doctrine indeed denies both the Father and the Son.

Response: The three weakest points of Oneness theology are as follows:

1. **The places where Jesus interacts with the Father** especially where He prays to the Father and where the Father loves Jesus (Matt. 3:16-17; Luke 10:21-22; John 10:17; 17:1ff.).
2. **The places in the OT and NT that teach the preexistence of the person of the Son** (the angel of the LORD appearances;

---

31 As defined by the UPCI authority and Oneness author, David Bernard in his most recognized book, *The Oneness of God* (1983), 99, 103, 252.

32 Cf. ibid., 103-4; Gordon Magee, *Is Jesus in the Godhead or Is The Godhead in Jesus?* (1988), 25.

33 Cf. *The Oneness of God*, 106, 122.

34 Cf. *The Oneness of God*, 57; T. Weisser, *Three Persons from the Bible? or Babylon* (1983), 2.

Gen. 19:24; Isa. 9:6; Dan. 7:9-14; Mal. 5:2 et al.; John 1:1; 3:13; 6:38; 16:28; 17:5; Phil. 2:6-11; Heb. 1:10-12; Rev. 1:8, 17; 2:8; 22:13). This would include the places that present the person of the Son as the Creator of all things (John 1:3, 10; Col. 1:16-17; *Heb. 1:2, 10-12*).

3. **The places that present the person of the Son as God, and distinct from God the Father** (*Mark 14:61-64;* John 1:1, 18; 5:17-18; 8:24, 58 et al.; 10:28-30; 17:5; Phil. 2:6-11; Titus 2:13[35]; *Heb. 1:6,* 8-12; 1 John 5:20; 2 John 1:3; Rev. 5:13-14 et al.). Moreover, in NT, there are numerous passages where all three persons are shown as distinct from each other, either in the same passage or same context (esp. Matt. 28:19; Luke 10:21-22; 2 Cor. 13:14; Eph. 2:18; Titus 3:5-7; 1 Pet. 1:2; Jude 1:21-22). The NT explicitly teaches that Jesus is the "Son" of God, and not once is He called or identified as the "Father"[36] (cf. 2 John 1:3).

JEHOVAH'S WITNESSES[37]

The Jesus of the JWs, near identical to what Arius taught, is "a god" (John 1:1; NWT[38]), but not God almighty. They teach that Jesus was Michael, the created, archangel being the "firstborn" of Jehovah's works. They even use some of the same passages as did Arius to prove their position (e.g., Prov. 8:22; Col. 1:15; Rev. 3:14) in the same erroneous way.

As said, it is because of their prior theological commitment of unitarianism (God as one person) that they deny that Jesus Christ is truly God.[39] Further, the JWs deny the physical resurrection of Jesus Christ.

---

35 See note 124 in which Jesus as "the God" is grammatically affirmed at Titus 2:13 and 2 Peter 1:1.

36 Oneness advocates typically appeal to John 10:30 ("I and the Father are one"). However, as seen above in detail, this passage in its context systematically refutes the Oneness unitarian interpretation and positively affirms the distinction between the Jesus and the Father: "For this reason the Father loves Me, because I lay down My life so that I may take it back (John 10:17). For more information on John 10:30; 14:9 and other passages used by Oneness advocates to promote a unitarian Oneness God, see, *A Definitive Look at Oneness Theology: In the Light of Biblical Trinitarianism,* 4th ed. by Edward L. Dalcour >**www.christiandefense.org**<

37 The Watchtower Bible and Tract Society is the corporate name for the JWs.

38 As mentioned above, the NWT (The New World Translation) is the biblical translation of the JWs, published by the Watchtower.

39 In the Watchtower publication, *Should you Believe in the Trinity?*, the JWs are repetitiously taught that Jesus was merely "a god" who had a beginning as a created angel: The Bible is clear and consistent about the relationship of God to Jesus. Jehovah God alone is Almighty. He created the prehuman Jesus

According to the JWs, Jesus did not die on a cross, but rather was impaled on a torture stake as a sacrifice for sins, but only as a "ransom payment" for the sins of Adam.[40] In this view, the biblical teaching of the atonement is wholly robbed and denied of its efficacy.

Response: The chief heresy of the JWs is the denial of the Trinity and thus, a denial of Jesus Christ as God in the flesh. As seen, the deity of the Son is a constant theme in the NT (as seen above). Unless one believes that the Son is the "I am," that is, *I am the eternal God;*[41] he or she will die in his or her sins (John 8:24).

Aside from Proverbs 8:22,[42] most JWs appeal to Colossians 1:15 First We also saw the vast number of passages that clearly identified Jesus as YHWH, not merely in representation, but rather in an ontological sense. And many of these OT references were not merely speaking of the Son in prophecy, but rather in actual preexistence, that is, personally interacting with others (e.g., Gen. chaps. 18-19;

---

directly. Thus, Jesus had a beginning and could never be coequal with God in power or eternity (*Should you Believe in the Trinity?: Is Jesus Christ the Almighty God?* [Watchtower Bible and Tract Society, 1989], 16).

40 The Watchtower position is clear: "Since one man's sin (that of Adam) had been responsible for causing the entire human family to be sinners, the shed blood of another perfect human (in effect, a second Adam), being of corresponding value, could balance the scales of justice" (*Reasoning from the Scriptures* [Watchtower Bible and Tract Society, 1989], 308).

41 In the LXX, there are several places where YHWH claims to be the (unpredicated) *egō eimi* ("I am"; Deut. 32:39; Isa. 41:4; 43:10; and 46:4), as seen, Christ made the same claims of Himself (Matt. 14:27; Mark 6:50; John 6:20; 8:24, 28, 58; 13:19; 18:5, 6, 8).

42 The NWT reads: "Jehovah produced me as the beginning of his way. The earliest of his achievements of long ago." The JWs are taught that this passage teaches that Jesus was created. In refutation:

   1. Even if the passage was referring to Christ, as some see it, it does not support the JW unitarian position that Christ was created. As seen, the Scripture positively affirms the eternal preexistence and true deity of the person of the Son (Dan. 7:13-14; John 1:1,3, 18; 8:24, 58 et al., 17:5; Phil. 2:6-11; Col. 1:16-17; Heb. 1:10-12; Rev. 1:8; 22:13).

   2. The context of chapters 1-9 is wisdom, which is personified as a female (cf. 8:2; 9:1, 2, 3). It would be problematic to apply a female personification to the Messiah. Nowhere in the OT nor NT is this done.

   3. Since chapters 1-9 are contextually speaking of wisdom, then the reading: "Jehovah produced me as the beginning of his way," would prompt the question to JWs: Was there a time when Jehovah was without wisdom? Moreover, note that the phrase in 8:23: "From everlasting I was established" denotes eternality (similar phrase in Ps. 90:2). So, even if 8:22 is a description of Christ, it actually proves that He is eternal.

   4. The word translated "produced" ("Jehovah himself produced me") is from the Hebrew term *quanah*. While *qanah* carries a several meanings, the primary meaning is *to acquire, buy, purchase, possess* as seen especially throughout the book of Proverbs (1:5; 4:5; 15:32; 16:16; 17:16; 19:8; 20:14, etc.). The meaning of "create," although possible (cf. BDB, Thayer), is rarely used in this way. The TLOT Lexicon points out that the Hebrew term may be used "in relation to birth cf. Psa 139:13 ["formed"] and perhaps Prov 8:22." In this sense, Proverbs 8:22 may be speaking of the birth of Christ (incarnation, viz. His humanity, not deity), same sense is found in Psalm 22:10: "I was cast upon You from birth; You have been my God from my mother's womb."

the angel of the LORD references, as shown above; Dan. 7:13-14). Additionally, specific titles and attributes were applied to Jesus in the NT, which were either exclusively applied to YHWH/God in the OT or unequivocally signified the Son's ontological identification as truly God. For example,

The person of Jesus Christ is presented as:

- **"Lord over all"** (Acts 10:36).
- **Son of God** (Mark 1;1; 14:61-14; John 5:17-18).
- **Son of Man** (Dan. 7:13-14; Mark 10:45; 14:61-64; John 6:53; 8:28; 9:35-37 et al.).
- **"God over all"** (Rom. 9:5, NET).
- **"The Lord of glory"** (1 Cor. 2:8; cf. 1 Sam. 15:29; Acts 7:2).
- **Always existing (subsisting) in the nature of God** (Phil. 2:6).
- **Always dwelling all the fullness of Deity in bodily form** (Col. 2:9).
- **The Creator of all things** (John 1:3; Col. 1:16-17; Heb. 1:10-12).
- **"Savior"** (Titus 2:13-14; 2 Pet. 3:18; cf. Isa. 45:21; Hosea 13:4).
- **The only means of salvation** (faith in Him, apart from works; John 3:14-18; 6:47; 11:25-26; Rom. 4:4-8; 5:1; 8:1; Eph. 1:4-5; 1 John 5:12 et al.).
- **The *Monogenēs Theos*** ("unique, one and only, God").
- **"The great God"** (Titus 2:13; cf. 2 Pet. 1:1- Ps. 95:3).
- The ***Ho ōn*** ("who is," lit., "The One, timelessly existing" (John 1:18; Rom. 9:5; Rev. 1:8).
- **"The only Master and Lord"** (Jude 1:4).
- **"The true God"** (1 John 5:20; cf. 2 Chron. 15:3; Jer. 10:10).
- **The YHWH of Psalm 102-25-27** (cf. Heb. 1:10-12); **Isaiah 6:1-10** (cf. John 12:39-41); **Isaiah 8:12-13** (cf. 1 Peter 3:14-15); **Isaiah 45:23** (cf. Phil. 2:10-11); **Joel 2:32** (cf. Rom. 10:13) et al.

The Father *directly addressed* the Son as,

- **"The God"** whose throne is eternal (Heb. 1:8-9) and the **"Lord"** (viz., the YHWH) of Psalm 102:25-17, the unchangeable Creator (Heb. 1:10-12; cf. John 1:3; Col. 1:16-17).

Jesus claimed to be,

- **Son of God** (John 5:17-18; Mark 14:61-64 et al.).
- **"Son of Man"** (Dan. 7:13-14; Mark 10:45; 14:61-64; John 6:53; 8:28; 9:35-37 et al.).
- The **"I am"** (Mark 6:50; John 8:24, 28, 58 et al.; cf. Deut. 32:39; Isa. 41:4; 43:10; 46:4).
- **"Equal with God"** (John 5:17-18; 10:30-33).
- **"The Alpha and Omega"** and the **"First and the Last"** (Rev. 1:8, 17; 2:8; 22:13; cf. Isa. 41:4; 44:6; 48:12; cf. Dan. 7:14).

Jesus was,

- **Worshiped in a religious context, thus, as God:** (Matt. 14:33; John 9:38; *Heb. 1:6;* Rev. 5:13-14).
- **Preexisting together *with* the Father, and shared glory *with* Him, "before the world existed"** (John 17:5).

JWs neither confess that Jesus is YHWH nor do they believe that He was physically resurrected from the dead: **"This [the Son] is the true God and life eternal"** (1 John 5:20).

THE CHURCH OF JESUS CHRIST OF LATTER-DAY SAINTS (LDS, I.E., MORMONISM)

Aside from the countless theological distortions, the main fundamental difference between biblical Christianity and LDS doctrine is simply (ontological) monotheism, that is, there exists one true God (monotheism) by nature.

The LDS chief doctrines: Eternal Progression and Exaltation: *eternal progression* is the so-called progression that man experiences: First, there is man's "preexistence" before coming to earth, or what Mormons call, "first estate." All men were existing in heaven as the literal spirit children of God the Father and one of His wives, by sexual relations. After which, they are sent to earth to receive their physical bodies (i.e., mortality), which is called, in LDS terminology, the "second estate." Then when people here on earth die, they go first to the "spirit world" to await their final destination, which will be one of the three levels of heavens: *celestial, terrestrial* or the *telestial* being the lowest. Thus, *eternal progression* is the process from preexistence to earth then to the final abode, which is one of the three heavens, or hell, if one becomes a "sons of perdition."[43]

The LDS doctrine of *exaltation* simply means *man becoming God*. LDS Apostle Lorenzo Snow, who later became the fifth President of the Church sums up the LDS man-to-God doctrine in a short couplet, which has been constantly quoted by LDS leaders: **"As man now is, God once was; as God now is, man may become."** In LDS theology then, men and God are of the "same species." The LDS doctrine *exaltation* teaches then that God the Father was a mere man that had to become a God. As we will see clearly below the LDS Church does not hold to the biblical teaching that God the Father (or the Son) existed eternally as God, rather the LDS holds to the false notion that God became God at a certain point in time by obedience to His Father, back on another planet similar to earth. So, the LDS doctrine of *eternal progression* is the progression of man's journey to Godhood and *exaltation* is the LDS doctrine of man exalting to God.

Founder and so-called, prophet, Joseph Smith declared:

I will preach on the plurality of Gods ... I have always and in all congregations when I have preached on the ... subject of Deity, it has been the plurality of Gods.... God the Father, and that the Holy Ghost ... these three constitute three distinct personages and three Gods."[44]

The LDS denies the concept of an eternal God, rather

[God] was once a man like us; yea, that God himself, the Father of us all, dwelt on an earth, the same as Jesus Christ himself did.... and you have got to learn how to be Gods yourselves ... the same as all Gods have done before you."[45]

---

43 *Sons of perdition* in LDS doctrine are the devil and his angels and those who understand LDS theology and teach and/or speak out against it.
44 *Teachings of the Prophet Joseph Smith* (Deseret Book Co, Salt Lake City, UT: The Church of Jesus Christ of Latter-day Saints, 1989), 370.
45 Ibid., 345-47.

Therefore, in LDS theology, neither Jesus nor the Father are eternal God—rather, they both had to become God by obedience to their God. Also, the LDS Jesus was married to Mary and Martha.[46] Further, the LDS teach that Jesus was "begotten" by means of sexual relations between God the Father and the Virgin Mary. For example:

LDS President, Brigham Young: "The birth of the Savior was as natural as are the births of our children; it was the result of natural action ... was begotten of his Father, as we were of our fathers...."[47]

LDS Apostle and scholar Bruce R. McConkie:

Christ was begotten by an Immortal Father in the same way that mortal men are begotten by mortal fathers.... as the literal Son ... he was born in the same personal, real, and literal sense that any mortal son is born to a mortal father. There is nothing figurative about his paternity.[48]

Response: The chief essential heresies of LDS theology, 1) God is not eternal and was a mortal man that had to become a God, 2) there exist many true Gods, and 3) God is an exalted man with a body parts and sexual passions for His wife (or wives) and Mary, the mother of Jesus.

The One true eternal God by nature

As pointed out in note 22 above, technically, the LDS Church is *henotheistic* believing that although many true Gods/gods exist, worship and devotion is to only the one God of this planet. Of course, it's still a pagan *polytheistic* (many true Gods) system.

OT revelation:

- **Deuteronomy 6:4:** "Hear, O Israel: The LORD our God, the Lord is one."

---

46 Cf. LDS Apostle Orson Hyde, *Journal of Discourses*, 2:10, 81-82; 4:259; LDS Apostle Orson Pratt, *The Seer,* 158-59; LDS Apostle who became President, *Wilford Woodruff in Wilford Woodruff's Journal* 8:187, July 22, 1883.

47 *Journal of Discourses*, 8:115.

48 Bruce R. McConkie, *Mormon Doctrine* (1966 ed.), 546-47, 742.

- **Isaiah 43:10:** "'You are My witnesses,' declares the LORD, 'and My servant whom I have chosen, So that you may know and believe Me and understand that I am He [*egō eimi*, "I am," LXX]. Before Me there was no God formed, and there will be none after Me.'"
- **Isaiah 44:6, 8:** "I am the first and I am the last; apart from Me [singular] there is no God.... ⁸ You are my witnesses. Is there any God besides me? No, there is no other Rock; I know not one" (cf. also Deut. 4:35; Ps. 100:3; Isa. 44:24; 45:5).
- ***Jeremiah 10:10-11:*** "But the LORD is the true God; He is the living God and the everlasting King. The earth quakes at His wrath, and the nations cannot endure His indignation. ¹¹ This is what you shall say to them: 'The gods that did not make the heavens and the earth will perish from the earth and from under these heavens.'"

NT revelation:

- **Mark 12:29-30:** "Jesus answered, 'The foremost is, "Hear, Israel! The Lord is our God, the Lord is one; ³⁰ and you shall love the Lord your God with all your heart, and with all your soul, and with all your mind, and with all your strength.'"
- **1 Corinthians 8:4-6:** "Therefore, concerning the eating of food sacrificed to idols, we know that an idol is nothing at all in the world, and that there is no God but one. ⁵ For even if there are so-called gods whether in heaven or on earth, as indeed there are many gods and many lords, ⁶ yet for us there is *only* one God, the Father, from whom are all things, and we *exist* for Him; and one Lord, Jesus Christ, by whom are all things, and we *exist* through Him."
- **Galatians 4:8:** "However at that time, when you did not know God, you were slaves to those which by nature are not gods."
- **1 Timothy 2:5:** "For there is one God, and one mediator also between God and mankind, the man Christ Jesus."

God is an omnipresent spirit, not flesh and bones, as the LDS teaches.⁴⁹

---

49 Joseph Smith originally taught that God is spirit (cf. Smith's, *Lectures of Faith,* sec. V; Book of Mormon (Alma 31:15; 22:10 et al.). Smith changed his doctrine from God is spirit to God is an exalted man with body parts and sexual passions later in life.

- **2 Chronicles 6:18:** "The heavens, even the highest heavens, cannot contain You" (cf. also Jer. 23:24).
- **Hosea 11:9:** "I am God and not a man" (lit. "God I am and not man," cf. Num. 23:19, lit. "Not a man is God").
- **John 1:18: "No one has ever seen God**, but God the One and Only, who is at the Father's side has made him known" (cf. 1 John 4:12).[50]
- **John 4:24:** "God is spirit." In Luke 24:39, Jesus defines a spirit, "a spirit does not have flesh and bones as you see I have."
- **Colossians 1:15:** "He [Jesus] is the image of the **invisible** [*aoratou*] God...."
- **1 Timothy 1:17:** "Now to the King eternal, immortal, **invisible** [*aoratō*], the only God...."
- **1 Timothy 6:16:** "who alone is immortal and who lives in unapproachable light, whom no one has seen or **can** [*dunamai*, 'has the ability to'] see."

God has *always been* God for eternity

- **Psalm 90:2:** "Before the mountains were born or You gave birth to the earth and the world, even from everlasting to everlasting, You are God."
- **Psalm 74:12:** "Yet God is my King from long ago, who performs acts of salvation in the midst of the earth."
- **1 Timothy 1:17:** "Now to the eternal king, immortal, invisible, the only God, be honor and glory forever and ever! Amen."
- **Hebrews 1:12:** "and like a robe You [the Son] will fold them up and like a garment they will be changed, but You are the same and Your years will never run out" (cf. Heb. 1:10-11).

---

50 John 1:18 is so contradictive to LDS theology that in the so-called *Joseph Smith's Translation* (JST, also called the *Inspired Version*) he altered the actual words of the Apostle John (v. 19 in the JST): "And no man hath seen God at any time, **except he hath borne record of the Son;** for except it is through him no man can be saved" (emphasis added).

SEVEN

Conclusion

Jesus said that true worshipers of God will worship Him "in spirit and truth" (John 4:24). We must honor God in our doctrine correctly proclaiming the Son in spirit and truth. Christians are called to "honor the Son even as they honor the Father. He who does not honor the Son does not honor the Father who sent Him" (John 5:23). By proclaiming the person of the Son as God, we honor both the Father and the Son, thus we worship God in spirit and truth. The OT and NT are the earliest revelation of God. Then why are there so many views of God and who Jesus is? ***Three chief reasons:***

1. **Prior theological assumptions or commitments.** Those who deny the Trinity and the deity of Christ typically deny it on the basis of their own prior theological assumption, rather than engaging in a proper exegetical (basic) study of Scripture. For example, Muslims, Oneness believers, and JWs reject the Trinity (generally misrepresenting it as three Gods) because of their assumed conclusion that God is unipersonal, before actually proving it. Further, the prior theological assumptions of liberal scholarship (e.g., the Jesus Seminar) hold to a *naturalistic assumption,* which states that since the beginning

of time everything has happened naturally. Therefore, their argument starts with an unproven philosophical conclusion: there has never been (or will be) divine supernatural events such as the biblically recorded miracles especially the physical resurrection of Jesus Christ. It is from this unproven starting point that the biblical reliability is rejected.

2. **A faulty hermeneutic and flawed exegesis.** Every heresy (false teaching) starts with a faulty exegesis ("to lead out"). Exegesis is the method of achieving the biblical authors' "intended" meaning of a biblical text by critically analyzing its grammar, context, and historical setting. We are never to engage in eisegesis ("to lead into," thus, reading into the text one's own presupposition). Without proper exegesis, one can make the Bible say whatever he or she would like it to say. Exegesis protects the authors' intended meaning—especially, against heresy. The Christian exegete comes to the Bible with the belief that the Bible is the word of God, infallible and inerrant. Scripture is the starting point of all theological assertions, and,

3. **No ability to hear—John 8:47:** "The one who is of God hears the words of God; for this reason, you do not hear them, because you are not of God." The unregenerate man cannot hear the words of God. He is dead (Eph. 2:1-4) having no ability to come to God (John 6:44). Neither does the unsaved man have the ability to submit to God nor please Him, he is "not even able *to do so*" (Rom. 8:7-8). **It is the gospel proclamation that is the power of God for salvation** (Rom. 1:16). In the OT and NT Scripture presents a tri-personal God. There is one God; there are three distinct coequal coeternal coexistent self-cognizant divine persons or *Egos* that share the nature of the one God—the Father, the Son, and the Holy Spirit. **The Trinity is God's chief revelation to mankind. Jesus Christ, the Son of God, is presented as the two natured person.** He was the YHWH who "Rained on Sodom and Gomorrah, brimstone and fire from YHWH out from heaven" (Gen. 19:24). Jesus Christ unambiguously claimed to be God, the Son of Man, the YHWH of the OT, while affirming His distinction from His Father and the Holy Spirit.

Biblical apologetics is the act of defending (and affirming) the gospel of Jesus Christ, the Christian Faith—that was *hapax* ("once for all time") delivered to the saints, for which all Christians are called to contend earnestly (Jude 1:3). 1 Peter 3:15 mandates all Christians "to sanctify Jesus Christ as Lord" and be ready to give a defense and an answer for the Christian faith (cf. 2 Cor. 10:3-5; Titus 2:13). All Christians are called by God to boldly proclaim the gospel of Jesus Christ and oppose all who come against fundamental Christian doctrines. Apologetics glorifies Christ, as Christ Himself celebrated the pastors of the church of Ephesus for laboring in practicing apologetics (Rev. 2:1-3). Because of the false teachers "speaking perverse things" within the church, for three years, Paul admonished the Ephesian pastors, night and day with tears, to "Be on guard for yourselves and for all the flock." The mandated biblical responsibility of Christian pastors is to guard and *shepherd* the flock, and confront, and sharply refute unbiblical teachings (Titus 1:9. 13).

All Christians should not be afraid of the task of defending and affirming biblical truth. So, in Galatians 1:10, Paul asks, "For am I now seeking the favor of men, or of God? Or am I striving to please men? If I were still trying to please men, I would not be a bond-servant of Christ." That should be the attitude of all faithful Christians: *Defend and affirm the faith boldly!*

> [3] "For though we walk in the flesh, we do not wage battle according to the flesh, [4] for the weapons of our warfare are not of the flesh, but divinely powerful for the destruction of fortresses. [5] We are destroying arguments and all arrogance raised against the knowledge of God, and we are taking every thought captive to the obedience of Christ" (2 Cor. 10:3-5).

APPENDIX A

The deity and unipersonality of the Holy Spirit

1. He was called "God" and "Lord" in a religious context.
2. He was identified as YHWH.
3. He possesses divine attributes.
4. The Holy Spirit accomplishes divine works.
5. He was worshiped as God; that is, in *the same way* as that of the Father (and Son).
6. He possesses personal attributes and characteristics affirming His personhood.
7. The Holy Spirit is a distinct person from the Father and the Son.

BIBLICAL DATA

1. As with the Son, the Holy Spirit was referred to as God and Lord in a religious context.

The biblical authors, who were strict monotheists, present the Holy Spirit as truly God distinct from the Father and the Son.

The Holy Spirit was referred to as *Theos* ("God," Acts 5:3-4). In the Ananias and Sapphira narrative (Acts 5:1-5), the personhood of the Holy Spirit is unquestionably seen by the fact that only a self-aware subject (i.e., person) can be lied to—one cannot lie to a rock or electricity. In verse 4, however, the person of the Holy Spirit, to whom Ananias lied, is called "God" (*Theos*). For after Peter had harshly asked Ananias, "why has Satan filled your heart to lie to the Holy Spirit?" Peter had then explained in the next verse, "You [Ananias] have not lied to men but to God." Also, in the narrative, the Holy Spirit is called, "the Spirit of the Lord." "Then Peter said to her, 'Why is it that you have agreed together to put the Spirit of the Lord to the test?'" (Acts 5:9). In the OT, the phrase, "the Spirit of the Lord [YHWH]" occurs two-dozen times. "The Spirit of YHWH" was indeed YHWH.

He was called Lord (*Kurios*) in a religious context (2 Thess. 3:5). As mentioned above, the NT authors quoted OT passages referring to YHWH and applied them to the Holy Spirit. The person of the Holy Spirit is referred to both God and Lord in a religious context, thus, ontologically (in essence).

2. Identified as YHWH.

In the OT, the Spirit of God was God. David rhetorically asks YHWH, "Where can I go from Your Spirit? Or where can I flee from Your presence?" (Ps. 139:7). The Hebrew parallelism here indicates that David sees YHWH's Spirit as the very presence of YHWH. Further, throughout the OT, the "Spirit" (or "Spirit of YHWH" or "Spirit of God") shares the same attributes as YHWH. For example, He is said to be the Creator (Gen. 1:2; Job 33:4; Ps. 104:30); He abides with believers (Ps. 51:11; Isa. 63:10-11); He gives wisdom, understanding, and knowledge to men (Exod. 31:3).

As said, the NT authors cite OT passages referring to YHWH and apply them to the Holy Spirit (e.g., Acts 28:25-27, Heb. 3:7; 10:15; also cf. Acts 5:9 with Deut. 6:16).

3. The Holy Spirit possesses divine attributes.

As God, the Holy Spirit possesses the specific attributes that only God has. The author of Hebrews indicates that the Holy Spirit is eternal: "How much more will the blood of Christ, who through the eternal Spirit offered Himself without blemish to God, cleanse your conscience from dead works to serve the living God" (Heb. 9:14). The author of Hebrews also refers to the Spirit as *pneumatos aiōniou* (lit.), "Spirit eternal." The same adjective (*aiōniou,* "eternal") is used of God in Rom. 16:26: *Theou aiōniou,* "God eternal." Thus, the person of the Holy Spirit is the eternal God—for only God is eternal.

4. The Holy Spirit accomplishes divine works.

For example, the Holy Spirit is the *agent* of Mary's pregnancy (Matt. 1:18); He regenerates a spiritually dead man (John 3:5; Titus 3:5); He dwells in/with the believer (1 Cor. 3:16); distributes spiritual gifts according to His own will (1 Cor. 12:11); seals believers for redemption (Eph. 1:13); and sanctifies believers and works in their lives (Thess. 2:13). Only because the Holy Spirit is God, omnipotent, omniscient, and omnipresent is He able to complete these acts. Moreover, Paul says in 1 Corinthians 2:10 that the Holy Spirit "searches all things even the depths of God." The Greek term translated "searches" is *erauna* (from *ereunaō*). This verb carries the idea of "logical investigation" (BDAG). The tense indicates that the "searching" is continuous and active—He is always searching, knowing all things at all times. In verse 11, the Holy Spirit is said *to know* the thoughts of God. Only God can know the thoughts of God.

5. He was worshiped as God; that is, in the same way as that of the Father (and Son).

In Matthew 28:19, Jesus commands all new converts to be baptized into the name (i.e., "power, authority") of the triune God. Water baptism signifies the unification or identification with whom the participant is being baptized—the Father, and the Son, and the Holy Spirit. Another kind of religious worship is direct prayer. In Matthew 9:38, Jesus instructs His disciples to "beseech the Lord of the harvest to send out workers into His harvest." First, the fact that Jesus refers to "Lord of the harvest" in the third person ("His", not "My" harvest) indicates that the "Lord of the harvest" is not Himself. Second, as seen, the Holy Spirit is called "Lord" several times in the NT *in a religious context.* Third, there is no contextual reason to believe that the "Lord of the harvest" is the Father. And finally, in Acts 13:1-4, the Holy Spirit sends out the laborers ("Barnabas and Saul") to the missionary (harvest) field. As God, the Holy Spirit was worshiped and honored in the same sense as that of the Father and Christ.[1]

6. He possesses personal attributes and characteristics affirming His personhood.

As seen, groups such as the JWs reject the personhood of the Holy Spirit—seeing the Holy Spirit as an impersonal force, like electricity. The personhood of the Holy Spirit is biblically demonstrated and defined by **(a) personal pronouns and first-person verbs applied to Him** and **(b) He possesses personal attributes.** In fact, the same biblical data that supports the personhood of God the Father is applied to the Holy Spirit.

(a) *Personal pronouns and first person verbs.* In the NT, personal pronouns are applied to the Holy Spirit. In Acts 10:19-20, for example, the Holy Spirit identifies Himself, not merely as "God's activity," but rather as *egō* ("I"), that is, a self-aware person:

> [19] "While Peter was reflecting on the vision, the Spirit said to him, "Behold, three men are looking for you. [20] But get up, go downstairs and accompany them without misgivings, for I [*egō*] have sent them Myself."

And in Acts 13:2, we read: "While they were serving the Lord and fasting, the Holy Spirit said, 'Set Barnabas and Saul apart for **Me** for the work to which **I have called them.**'" Here the Holy Spirit not only issues (communicates) personal commands, but refers to Himself as *moi* ("Me," from *egō*) and uses the first-person verb *proskeklēmai* ("I have called them")—this verb is only used of persons in the NT.

(b) *Personal attributes and Characteristics.* Personal attributes and characteristics. It would be a fallacy of equivocation to equate person with people, as many anti-trinitarians do. Those who do so misunderstand the meaning of both terms. For example, angels fall under the category of "person," but they are not "people." Likewise, the Holy

---

1   As shown above, in a religious context, *Kurios* ("Lord") carries the same semantic equivalence as *Theos* ("God").

Spirit can be called and ontologically categorized as "person," though He is not in the ontological class of "people" (same with the Father). So, all people are persons, but not all persons are people. Hence, God the Father, Satan, demons, angels, and the Holy Spirit are persons, but they are not people.

The Holy Spirit possesses many personal characteristics (as with the Father and Son) denoting that the Holy Spirit is a self-aware subject or Ego (i.e., person) cognizant of His own existence, which is clearly demonstrated by the specific personal characteristics or attributes He possesses:

- He can be blasphemed (Mark 3:29, 30).
- He can be lied to (Acts 5:3).
- He intercedes or prays on the behalf of the believer (Rom. 8:26).
- He issues commands (Acts 13:2, 4; 16:6).
- He is intelligent in that He investigates and searches (1 Cor. 2:10-11; Rom. 8:27).
- He has a will (1 Cor. 12:9-11).
- He can be grieved (Isa. 63:10; Eph. 4:30).
- He testifies (Neh. 9:30; John 15:26; Heb. 10:15) and teaches (John 14:26).

Only cognizant persons can exercise and engage in intelligent communication (Acts 10:19-20; 13:2, 4). Scripture presents many clear examples of the Holy Spirit intelligently communicating to others (1 Kings 22:24; John 16:13; Acts 8:29; 10:19-20; 13:2; 28:25, 26; Heb. 3:7-11; 10:15-17). Even the anti-trinitarian JWs in the Watchtower's *Awake* magazine distinguish a personification from a person, as they rightfully define a person: "Is the Devil a personification or a person? Can an unintelligent person carry on a conversation with a person? ... only an intelligent person can."[2] The Apostle Paul, in his Trinitarian benediction, comforts the saints in Corinth with these words: **"The grace of the Lord Jesus Christ, and the love of God, and the fellowship of the Holy Spirit be with you all"** (2 Cor. 13:14).

Only self-aware persons can experience true *koinōnia* ("fellowship"). This same *koinōnia,* believers have with the Father and the Son (1 John

2   *Awake!,* 8 December 1973, 27.

1:3). Moreover, as a distinct person, the Holy Spirit gives love: "Now I urge you, brethren, by our Lord Jesus Christ and *by the love of the Spirit,* to strive together with me in your prayers to God for me" (Rom. 15:30; emphasis added). Love is something that the Holy Spirit possesses and gives. As with true personal fellowship, only persons can possess, give, and experience love. Hence, abstract things such as natures, modes, manifestations, electricity, etc. have not the ontological capability to accomplish these things—only persons do. Thus, He is a person, not a mere influence.

7. *The Holy Spirit is a* distinct person *from God the Father and the Son.*

As with the Son (Matt. 28:19; Luke 10:21; Rom. 15:16; 2 Cor. 13:14; Eph. 2:18; 4:4-6; 2 Thess. 2:13; Titus 3:5-7), the Holy Spirit is frequently juxtaposed *with* the Father and the Son (Matt. 28:19—united by the "name"—namely, power and authority, cf. 1 Sam. 17:45). In Matthew 28:19 and 1 Corinthians 13:14, the persons in the Trinity are contextually and grammatically distinct. According to the rules of Greek grammar, when the Greek conjunction *kai* ("and") is inserted between nouns of the same case and each of those nouns are preceded by the article *ho* ("the") each noun denotes "a different person, thing, or quality from the preceding noun."[3] This construction is known as Granville Sharp rule #6[4]:

- **Matthew 28:19:** "Go, therefore, and make disciples of all the

---

3 Granville G. Sharp, *Remarks on the Uses of the Definite Article in the Greek Text of the New Testament,* 3rd ed. (London, UK: Vernor & Hood, 1803), 14-19.

4 This rule is named after its founder (not inventor) Granville Sharp (1735-1813). Sharp was passionate in his unyielding belief in the full deity of Jesus Christ. Sharp's research of the Greek NT led him to discover six grammatical rules in which the Greek article *ho* ("the") and the conjunction *kai* ("and") were utilized. The validity of the *six grammatical rules* discovered by Sharp were limited within the specifications of the rule itself. For example, according to Sharp, rule #1, when the Greek connective conjunction, *kai* ("and") connects two nouns of the same case (singular nouns that are not proper [e.g., personal names]), and the article *ho* ("the") precedes the first noun, but not the second, each descriptive noun refers to the first named person (cf. Sharp, 3-7). We see this construction in Titus 2:13 and 2 Peter 1:1: "The God and Savior, Jesus Christ." The two nouns "God" and "Savior" (in the same case and connected by "and") are governed by the one article, "the"—thus, both nouns refer to the first named person, "Jesus Christ" (Titus 2:13: *tou megalou Theou kai Sōtēros hēmōn Christou Iēsou,* lit., "The great God and Savior of us, Christ Jesus"; 2 Pet. 1:1: *tou Thou hēmōn kai Sōtēros Iēsou Christou,* lit., "The God of us and Savior, Jesus Christ"). The same construction found in 2 Peter 1:11; 2:20; and 3:18: "The Lord and Savior, Jesus Christ." According to Peter, Jesus is both "the God and Savior" and "the Lord and Savior."

nations, baptizing them in the name **of the** [*tou*] Father **and** [*kai*] **of the** [*tou*] Son **and** [*kai*] **of the** [tou] Holy Spirit."

- **2 Corinthians 13:14:** "The grace **of the** [*tou*] Lord Jesus Christ **and** [*kai*] the love **of the** [*tou*] God **and** [*kai*] the fellowship **of the** [*tou*] Holy Spirit be with all of you."[5]

Even more, the Son personally relates to the Father and to the person of the Holy Spirit; the reverse is altogether true of the Father and the Holy Spirit relating to each other. In John 14:16, Jesus said: "I will ask the Father, and He will give you **another** [*allon*] Helper ['Advocate' would be a better translation] that He may be with you forever." Therefore, Scripture presents that the Holy Spirit is a self-aware person or self. As a person, He possesses personal attributes and personal pronouns are applied to Him. The same evidence that confirms the personhood of the Father confirms the personhood of the Holy Spirit. Furthermore, Scripture clearly teaches that the Holy Spirit is God in the fullest and truest sense, being identified as YHWH. Accordingly, the Holy Spirit should be worshiped as God. He is distinct from the Father and the Son. He is the eternal almighty God, who regenerates sinners and glorifies the Father and the Son—**He is the Third Person of the Holy Trinity.**

---

5   Also 1 Thessalonians 3:11; 2 Thessalonians 2:16; 1 John 1:3; 2:22-23; and Revelation 5:13 contain Sharp's rule #6 constructions clearly differentiating the two persons—Jesus and God the Father.

APPENDIX B

John 1:1

In the beginning was the Word, and the Word was with God, and the Word was God.

En archē ēn ho Logos, Kai ho Logos ēn pros ton Theon, kai Theos ēn ho Logos, "In [the] beginning was the Word, and the Word was with the God, and God was the Word."

Grammatically, John 1:1 is divided in clauses, a, b, and c.

- **1:1a:** "In the beginning **was** the Word."
- **1:1b:** "and the Word was **with God**."
- **1:1c:** "and **the Word was God**."

John 1:1a indicates that the Word was eternally existing. The imperfect verb *ēn*[1] ("was") here, in this context (beginning of time)

---

1 *Ēn* is from the verb *eimi,* "I am, exist," "to be."

signifies a past ongoing action. Hence, no starting point of the Word's existence. So, in the beginning, the Word (*ēn*) "was" already existing.

John 1:1b indicates that the person of the Word was distinct from the Father: "the Word was **with** God [the Father]." The preposition *pros* ("face to face, towards, with"), applied to persons normally signifies intimate fellowship between person(s) (e.g., 2 Cor. 5:8: "but we are of good courage and prefer rather to be absent from the body and to be at home *pros ton Kurion* ['with the Lord']" (also see Rom. 5:1; 15:30; Eph. 2:18; 1 John 2:1 et al.).[2]

John 1:1c indicates that the Word was truly God.

1. *Theos* **in the** *emphatic position*. The Greek reads, *kai Theos ēn ho Logos* ("and God was the Word"). First, in Greek, the noun *Theos* ("God") is the **predicate nominative** (PN, explained below) and appears in front of the clause—namely, in the "emphatic position." This is a common feature in Greek. In other words, rather than placing a word in a clause according to firm grammatical function, placing a word in the emphatic position, would emphasize or draw attention to that word. The fact that *Theos* in John 1:1c is placed in the emphatic position makes it all more improbable for *Theos* to be translated as "indefinite" (one of many), as translated in the NWT of the JWs ("a god").

2. *Theos* **is the PN in the clause.** Grammatically, the PN is a noun in a clause or sentence that is in the same case (nominative) as that of the subject. A PN describes the larger category or state in which the subject belongs.[3] Here the PN in this clause (1:1c) is *Theos* and the subject is *Logos*—indicating that the Word belongs to the class or category (nature) of *Theos*, but is not the person of *ton Theon* ("the God," viz. the Father, 1:1b).

3. **Against Oneness theology: "God was the Word," not "*The* God was the Word."** The PN *Theos* is anarthrous (i.e., without the article, "the"), and comes before the verb (lit., "and God *was* the Word"). In this grammatical construction (viz. anarthrous preverbal

---

2   The prepositional phrase *pros ton Theon* ("with the God") occurs twenty times in the Greek NT. In each occurrence, *pros* differentiates between a person (s) and God, except three times where the neuter plural article *ta* ("the things"), which precedes the phrase: *ta pros ton Theon* ("the things pertaining to God"- at Rom. 15:17; Heb. 2:17; and 5:1). However, these three cases are not syntactically parallel to John 1:1b. For in John 1:1b, the imperfect verb *ēn* precedes the phrase–*ēn pros ton Theon* ("was with the God") unlike the three cases involving the neuter article *ta*.

3   GGBB, 40.

PN), the anarthrous PN is semantically qualitative[4] expressing essence, not identification or person. The lack of the article prevents any idea that the Word (Jesus Christ) was the same person of the Father. Now, if John had written, *Ho Theos ēn ho Logos* ("**The** God was the Word"), then he would be saying that "the Word" and "the God" (the Father) are the same person, since both nouns would be definite. But John did not write that.[5] Rather, John omits the article, which indicates that the PN *Theos* is *qualitative,* pointing to essence, not person: the Word in essence was God, but not the person of the Father. Definite nouns point to identification or person, while qualitative nouns point to nature or essence of something.[6] So Luther says, "the lack of an article is against Sabellianism; the word order is against Arianism."

Historically and contemporaneously, the Christian church and recognized biblical scholarship are roundly against the Arian (JWs) "a god" view and against the Oneness "the Word is the Father" view of John 1:1. John 1:1 teaches in the clearest way: The Word eternally existed (1:1a), He was *distinct* from the Father (1:1b), and in the same ontologically category of *Theos* (God), as to His nature, but not as the same person of the Father (1:1c). The content of the prologue (1:1- 18) tells us plainly that the person of the Word was truly God, that is, God the Son, the Creator of all things (cf. 1:3, 10, 18). This

---

4　Nouns generally fall under three semantic categories: *Definite* (identity), *Indefinite* (one in or of a class of others), or *Qualitative* (essence or nature—not identity, i.e., person). The anarthrous *Theos* in John 1:1c is qualitative. As with the noun "flesh" in John 1:14, "The Word became flesh," not "the flesh" (definite), or "a flesh" (indefinite), but "flesh" (qualitative)—as to the Word's new nature. Likewise, it would be most unnatural to translate *ho Theos agapē estin* in 1 John 4:8 (God is love) as "God is a love" (tagging *agapē* ["love"] as indefinite, "a love") or "God is the love" (definite, "the love"). Here *agapē* is qualitative. Grammatically, in John 1:1c, *Theos* is an anarthrous preverbal PN. A PN describes the class or category to which the subject (the "Word") belongs. Hence, the Word belongs to the category of *Theos* ("God") as to His essence—not His personal identity. A "definite" noun normally denotes identity, such as for example: the Lord, the Temple, Jerusalem, etc. or as with proper nouns: Paul, John, Jesus, Mary, etc. John 1:1b reads: *Kai ho Logos ēn pros ton Theon* ("the Word was with the God"). The articular (i.e., with the article, "the") noun *Theon* is a definite noun. It refers to the "person" of God the Father. Whereas in John 1:1c, the noun *Theos* (*kai Theos ēn ho Logos,* "and God was the Word") is qualitative pointing to essence, not identification or person.

5　Greek grammarian, Bill Mounce indicates that "When the article is present, it is emphasizing identity. When the article is not present, it is generally emphasizing the quality of the substantive" (Bill Mounce, *Basics of Biblical Greek Grammar* [Grand Rapids, MI: Zondervan, 2003], 334).

6　As shown above in note 70, there are no "viable" variants at John 1:1. There are only two late eighth century manuscripts, Codex Regius (L) and Codex Washingtonianus (W), which contain the articular *Theos* (*ho Theos,* "the God") at John 1:1c. However, as mentioned, this variant is seen as a non-viable variant meaning there is no legitimate likelihood of being an original reading.

has been affirmed not only by early patristics (pre-Nicene[7]), but by the vast majority of Christian scholarship.[8]

---

7   Ignatius (A.D. 107, *Letter to the Magnesians* 6); Justin Martyr (A.D. 150, *First Apology* 63); Irenaeus (A.D. 180, *Against Heresies* 4.20.1); Hippolytus (A.D. 205, *Against Noetus* 14); Tertullian (A.D. 213, *Against Praxeas* 3); Origen (A.D. 225, *First Principles* 4.1.30); Novatian (c. A.D. 256, "De Trinitate," in *Treatise of Novatian Concerning the Trinity* 18, 22, 23); Thaumaturgus, the Wonder-worker (A.D. 262, *A Sectional Confession of Faith* 7), and many more could be cited affirming the biblical-historic interpretation of John 1:1 in light of the concept of the Trinity.

8   Such as the Reformers, Puritans, Warfield, A. T. Robertson, Vincent, Dana-Mantey, Greeley, Vincent, Wallace, Reymond, Plumber, Meyer, Barns, Gill et al.